Rehearsing THE MIDDLE SCHOOL BAND

Stephen Meyer

Published by
Meredith Music Publications
a division of G.W. Music, Inc.
1584 Estuary Trail, Delray Beach, Florida 33483
http://www.meredithmusic.com

MEREDITH MUSIC PUBLICATIONS and its stylized double M logo are trademarks of
MEREDITH MUSIC PUBLICATIONS, a division of G.W. Music, Inc.

Reproducing or transmitting in any form or by any means, electronic or mechanical,
including photocopying, recording,
or by any informational storage or retrieval system without permission
in writing from the publisher is forbidden.

While every effort has been made to trace copyright holders and obtain permission,
this has not been possible in all cases; any omissions brought to our attention will be
remedied in future editions.

Copyright © 2018 MEREDITH MUSIC PUBLICATIONS
International Copyright Secured • All Rights Reserved
First Edition
October 2018

International Standard Book Number: 978-1-57463-485-3
Cataloging-in-Publication Data is on file with the Library of Congress.
Library of Congress Control Number: 2018958523
Printed and bound in U.S.A.

22   21   20   19   18   PP   1   2   3   4   5

Contents

Preface

"There is no elevator to success; you have to take the stairs."

One of my favorite shows to binge-watch on Netflix is called *Chef's Table*. This documentary series shares the personal journeys of world-renowned chefs and provides a glimpse into their creative genius. Although there are hundreds, perhaps thousands, of master chefs in the world, these individuals have overcome numerous hurdles in their path to success, yet they continue to revolutionize the culinary world. In the band profession, we also have pioneering educators to celebrate. My goal in writing *Rehearsing the Middle School Band* is to showcase twelve of the most prominent middle school, junior high, and elementary school band directors in the United States so that all can benefit from their experiences and successes.

Like the chefs on *Chef's Table*, these diverse master teachers have achieved an astounding level of musical excellence with their students and have received national and international recognition for their performances. They teach across the country in a variety of socioeconomic settings and in programs that are all very different from each other. Through hard work, perseverance, creativity, and an ongoing assessment of their programs, their students, and themselves, these consummate leaders have continually refined their craft, providing an exceptional experience for their students and redefining what is possible with young musicians. They are testament to the saying, "You cannot ride an elevator to success; you have to take the stairs."

Each chapter in this book is but an introduction to the wealth of knowledge these directors hold, focusing primarily on program structure, recruitment, curriculum, and rehearsal strategies for beginning musicians. The humorous and heartfelt anecdotes gleaned from our extended conversations reveal each director's sincere and ongoing passion for music education, but, just as in *Rehearsing the High School Band*, I regret that I could not possibly include everyone or everything. However, it is my hope that readers can apply the techniques shared within each chapter to their own programs, and that the creative ideas presented will spark similar innovations. I encourage readers to also look beyond these pages to seek out guidance and mentorship from experienced educators around them, as often our finest educators are the most generous with their knowledge. It may come as no surprise that those who have spent their careers tirelessly working for the betterment of music education are eager to impart their wisdom, insights, and lessons to other enthusiastic and dedicated band directors.

I am deeply grateful to these twelve directors for their willingness to be a part of this undertaking. Thank you to Garwood Whaley for his support of this project, Susan Gedutis Lindsay for her editorial assistance, and my family and friends for their continued love and encouragement.

—Stephen Meyer
Flagstaff, Arizona 2018

Kim Bain

"Good is the enemy of great."

Kim Bain is currently the director of bands at Louis Pizitz Middle School in Vestavia Hills, Alabama. She holds a bachelor of science in music education, a master of arts in music education, and an education specialist degree from the University of Alabama. She also earned a master of music degree in saxophone performance from Bowling Green State University.

Program Structure

Kim Bain started her career as an assistant band director at Ravenna High School in Ravenna, Ohio. After a year, she moved back to Birmingham and was the director of bands at Tarrant Middle School for four years and Oak Mountain Middle School for six years. Bain was the director of bands at R.F. Bumpus Middle School in Hoover, Alabama for seven years before becoming director of bands at Pizitz Middle School in 2006, where she has been for more than twelve years.

Louis Pizitz Middle School is located outside of Birmingham, Alabama and has approximately 1,100 students enrolled in grades six through eight. Around 250 students participate in band. Bain and her assistant teach two heterogeneous classes of sixth-grade beginners, two concert bands, and jazz band. Band classes meet for fifty-two minutes each day, and the school is currently on a rotating schedule whereby each period meets on a different day of the week. For example, a class might meet during the first hour on Monday, the second hour on Tuesday, and the third hour on

Wednesday. "This schedule allows the teacher to see the kids when they are at their best at some time during the week," she said. Bain also teaches sectionals or individual lessons during a study period that occurs in conjunction with the lunch period.

The two concert bands perform at a schoolwide citizenship assembly every nine weeks as well as an assembly in conjunction with the choral department in December and May. They also have a winter concert, statewide Music Performance Assessment (MPA) in late February, a festival performance as part of a spring trip, and a spring concert. The jazz band performs at the winter and spring concerts, a local jazz festival, and a competition at the Birmingham Jazz Hall of Fame.

In late January, many of the students audition for the Alabama all-state band. They prepare two etudes, scales, and sight-reading throughout the first semester. In the spring, 90 percent of the students participate in a solo and ensemble contest organized by the state music organization. While solos are not required, Bain allows students to choose between performing a solo and continuing to submit individual practice records. She also motivates students to participate by offering a party at the end of the grading period. All students are invited to attend practice sessions with Bain during the study period and after school.

Instrumentation
Three factors determine a student's ensemble placement: attendance, overall grades, and behavior. To qualify for the top ensemble, symphonic band, students need to have demonstrated excellent attendance at rehearsal and events during their first and second years of study. They also need to have good grades in other classes, as this shows that they are prepared to work hard, though each student is considered on a case-by-case basis. "Students who struggle academically may not be able to handle the rigor of the top ensemble, while for others, playing in the top ensemble motivates them to study for their other classes." Behavior and demeanor also matter, she said. "Students in the top ensemble have to be mature, in control of themselves, and able to handle the responsibilities of the group."

Bain prefers to have three or four tubas in the symphonic band and balances the instrumentation from low voices to high voices. She typically has two or three euphoniums, seven or eight trombones, seven to nine trumpets, four or five horns, five or six alto saxophones, one or two tenor saxophones, one baritone saxophone, twelve to fourteen clarinets, two bassoons, two oboes, and ten or eleven flutes. These numbers have gradually increased over the years as beginning band classes have grown.

The setup of the symphonic band changes each year as Bain assesses the strengths and weaknesses of each section. She prefers to have the tubas on the conductor's right and on the edge of the back row, as it creates a richer ensemble sound in the performance hall. If Bain has talented French horn players, they will sit to her left with bells facing the audience. If they are not strong players, she will place the horns in the middle of the ensemble. Bain typically places flutes to her left in the front row, followed by the clarinets on her right. However, if the clarinet section is small, they will sit in the first row, and the flutes sit in the second row. "This creates a better woodwind balance by dampening the higher voices and allowing the clarinets to project without any obstruction," Bain said.

Additional Instruction
Fifty-minute sectionals are held before school since many students are also involved in after-school activities. Using funds collected from an elective fee and fundraising, Bain hires private teachers to provide additional instrument-specific instruction. Students take private lessons during their homeroom class or after school, and Bain allocates a portion of fundraising efforts to help motivated students who need financial assistance. In previous positions, Bain hired students from a local university to teach sectionals or lessons at a reduced rate.

Recruitment
Bain has a single feeder school, and recruitment starts in the first semester, when small chamber groups from the middle school perform in the lobby for the elementary school musical. In the second semester, elementary music classes have a karate-inspired recorder program, in which students receive colored prizes as they progress. Bain targets the more advanced students and sends them an invitation to join the band. In March, she visits the elementary school and gives all fifth-grade music classes a general overview and demonstration of the woodwind and brass instruments. The jazz band then performs at the elementary school in April, and fifth graders receive a special invitation to the spring concert at Pizitz with tickets for VIP seating.

3

Instrument selection occurs at the end of the fifth grade or the beginning of sixth grade. Two local music stores fund the event and hire local band directors and private instructors to test students. When choosing the right instruments for students, Bain and her colleagues assess the student's physical attributes and their personality. She said:

> If the top edge of a student's upper lip resembles a double-curved bow, commonly called a "Cupid's Bow," that student may have a difficult time playing the flute. For clarinet, students have to be comfortable with flattening their chin and producing a tone with no air pockets. We do not start oboe until later because personality drives that instrument. The most successful oboists are confident, intellectual, and not afraid to be themselves. French horn players have to be able to sing and match pitch. Our percussion instructor also works with each interested student to see if they have a steady pulse and to assess their keyboard skills.

Instructors rate the students on each instrument, but students also indicate their personal preference. For more popular instruments like saxophone and percussion, students provide a second choice. "We tell parents that playing saxophone or percussion is somewhat like being the quarterback on the football team; there can only be a few picked for the position," Bain said. The evening after the instrument fitting, Bain e-mails each beginner informing them of which instrument they have the privilege to play. She has approximately ninety beginners each year and carefully manages the instrumentation: six tubas, six euphoniums, ten to twelve trombones, nine to ten trumpets, two oboes, two bassoons, ten to twelve flutes, twelve saxophones, twelve percussionists, and as many clarinets and French horns as possible. "While I try to get as close to these numbers as I can, we strongly encourage students to choose an instrument they are going to enjoy practicing at home," said Bain. "This way, they are going to have more fun, work harder, and enjoy the experience much more."

Overall, it is important for Bain to find the right students and the right families to participate in the band program. She has nearly 100 percent retention each year because the program has developed a reputation in the community, and parents and students understand the balance between having fun and working hard. Bain further explained:

> Everybody can, and everybody should, learn to play an instrument at some level, but there is work involved. Unlike some of the other fine arts, each

student contributes and impacts the ensemble as a whole. Parents and students sign a contract that outlines the expectations for participation in the band program. We want to be upfront from the beginning that they will have a great time and learn a lot but being in the band is more than fifty-two minutes each day. Individual practice, sectionals, and sometimes private lessons are also part of the program. Our goal is to combine their talent with hard work, and that attracts a specific personality and type of student and family.

Beginning Band Curriculum

For the first seven weeks, the beginner classes split into brass, woodwind, and percussion sectionals. Bain loosely bases the curriculum on the Suzuki method in that students learn "sound before sight." Written notation is introduced once students have learned the first five notes and have a solid command of instrument assembly, posture, hand position, breathing technique, and embouchure placement. "We start where songs and melodies are introduced in the method book because if they know five notes, they can play the songs," added Bain. "If you start at the beginning with whole notes, it immediately bursts their bubble of excitement."

Beginners have their first concert in October, because Bain believes it is vital for the parents to see the early stages of the process and for the students to have success early on. At this point, the tone quality and articulation of each section are still developing, but students can already play simple melodies. Following the concert, the beginner classes combine into a full ensemble. Students continue to build their range, increase their skills in reading notes and rhythms, build technical coordination, and learn how to play at various dynamic levels. Bain's assistant leads the full ensemble rehearsal while Bain addresses individual issues. By the end of the first year, the majority of beginners have an extended range produced with a characteristic tone and have the facility to play and sight-read in several keys.

Bain tracks progress throughout the year with periodic assessments. Students record and submit assignments using online tools such as *SmartMusic* or *Essential Elements Interactive*. Students can also record themselves in a practice room using school-owned iPads or complete their pass-off assignments with Bain or with their private teacher. Bain also firmly believes that students should gain experience performing in front of their peers. Beginners will perform "student-choice tests" where they pick one exercise from an assignment that consists of four or five lines from the method book. In the concert and symphonic bands, students frequently perform excerpts from the concert repertoire. "Students have to get used to playing in front of others because that is what we ultimately do as musicians," she said.

Score Study and Rehearsal Preparation

Bain always studies a score with her students in mind, considering the technical challenges and inherent pitch problems that could arise. "You have to know the fundamental challenges of the instruments to anticipate problems," she said. Bain carefully studies sections with thinner textures and more exposed playing, as those need special attention at the middle-school level.

When preparing for rehearsal, Bain considers the overarching concepts she will need to teach and plans a warm-up routine that incorporates those elements. For example, if a piece is in compound meter, warm-up exercises are rehearsed using rhythms in compound meter. Bain rehearses from a global perspective to hear where the challenges occur and then separates the music into logical sections. The first section is broken down further, beginning with the melody players, then countermelody and accompaniment sections. Those groups play together, working to match tone quality, intonation, articulation, and style. Once each musical element matches, the full ensemble will play, and Bain balances the ensemble sound so that each priority is heard. Over time, Bain rehearses larger sections of the music but continues to address and refine conceptual issues and work for greater clarity and unification.

Bain believes the key to teaching middle school is pacing and having a thorough knowledge of the instruments. She said:

> I see many young teachers jump into the musical details too soon, when the students are still processing fundamental concepts. Many novice teachers do not understand the adolescent brain and are not in tune with whether the students are receiving the information we are trying to offer. Earlier in my career I used to teach bell-to-bell, but research shows that adolescents cannot focus for that long. We now know that the length of an adolescent learning cycle is about ten minutes. So now in rehearsal, I vary the activities, get off the podium more, or have them stand after ten or fifteen

minutes of intense, focused work. I believe this helps them re-center, and it makes our rehearsals more productive overall.

Tone

Bain believes it is important to develop a proper tone in the first nine weeks of instruction. As she tells her students, "In the beginning, there was tone." She begins with breathing exercises and daily reinforcement of how to create a proper embouchure. Students spend a significant amount of time on the mouthpiece or head joint doing call-and-response exercises with Bain modeling. Bain and her assistant also model a characteristic tone quality on every instrument—a skill that she said took years to develop. Additionally, she asks her students to describe good and bad sounds, and she continuously reminds them to always listen carefully and be aware of the sound they are producing.

Bain also stresses the value of playing on reliable equipment to produce a characteristic tone. She said that she did not reinforce this concept as stoutly as she should have early in her career, and her students suffered as a result. Once she provided a list of recommended instruments and convinced parents of the limitations of specific brands of instruments, the quality of student playing improved. She said:

> I recommend not calling other brands bad, just different. Directors have to guide and educate parents on the long-term value. For students who cannot afford the investment, we place them on school-owned auxiliary instruments like bass clarinet, bari sax, French horn, tuba, or euphonium.

Bain conducts daily checks on the quality and condition of instruments, valves, mouthpieces, and reeds, and she continually moves around the room fixing students and adjusting instruments as required. "You have to be hands-on, all the time, with the beginners. You have to get off the podium," she said. "It is the only way they are going to get the individual attention they need to get better." As motivation, Bain gives out awards each day. For example, the "Golden Stand Award" is given to the student with the best tone quality. "We spray-painted a music stand gold, and that student gets to use it for the day," remarked Bain. "We make it an enormous privilege and give that student much praise for making characteristic sounds, with the hope that the other students will work just as hard to do the same."

Intonation

In Bain's elementary feeder program, students frequently sing simple melodies and learn solfege. She builds on these skills with her beginning band students, first introducing group singing while others play, then encouraging individual singing using incentives. For example, Pizitz has a school-wide reward system called "A-slips." Bain will give students A-slips if, for example, they can sing a concert F with no pitch reference or they can sing part or all of a melody in the method book. She said:

> I do whatever I can to get them over the fear of singing in front of each other. We have to be extremely encouraging, motivating, and make it okay to sing in any octave—especially since the seventh and eighth-grade boys are going through a voice change.

Once the physical setup of each student is correct, Bain gives a presentation to beginners on intonation and teaches them to identify out-of-tune wave frequencies. She uses a Yamaha Harmony Director keyboard to create extreme examples of unmatched frequencies, gradually moving the pitches together so students can hear the resulting waves. Bain also changes the timbre using various functions on the Harmony Director to demonstrate the difference between "in tone" and "in tune." Finally, towards the end of the first year, beginning students will complete a tuning tendency chart. She said:

> My goal is to train the ears, not the eyes. I ask many questions about what they hear to encourage listening, refine their aural awareness, and keep them engaged. Students are malleable and impressionable and can hear discrepancies, but only if we show them how.

Technique

Bain uses the *Essential Elements* series with both beginners and the two concert bands. She finds that the "technique trax" help engage students and make technical practice more engaging and exciting. The top ensemble also uses *Foundations for Superior Performance* to address advanced fundamentals such as extended diatonic and chromatic scales as well as lip and register slurs. In January, Bain begins a program called "JumpStart January," which focuses intensively on scales in preparation for the all-state auditions. Bain will test the student's ability to recall key signatures in a different order than the circle of fifths or fourths. For example, students will play a scale they know well, such as E-flat major, then immediately follow it with E major. The pattern continues with D-flat major and D major, B-flat major and B major, etc. "We have to use a variety of ways to present material to students who lack coordination and dexterity," said Bain. "For the woodwinds, this also means teaching alternate fingerings when we first introduce the notes."

With any technical assignment, Bain provides goal tempos for the end of the week and offers incentives if played correctly at even faster tempos. She said:

> Directors must provide differentiated instruction and go beyond the daily call of duty to keep students working. With passages that are technically challenging, create a warmup based on a difficult pattern. Change the rhythm in what students are learning in the music or method book, so that it is fresh and you are not just doing mindless repetitions. Figure out what is preventing them from being successful and why it is hard for that particular student. The possibilities are endless.

During the second nine-week grading period, if students in the beginning band classes can play five scales from memory, they get to join the "lunch bunch." Instead of eating lunch in the cafeteria, they get the privilege of eating in the band room. Bain also has a "March Madness" competition, in which the student that passes off the most exercises in the method book wins a prize. In seventh and eighth grade, students that pass-off all twelve major scales get to sign the "Pizitz Scale Fish"—a fifteen-pound bass fish that hangs above the entrance of the band room. "It has become a tradition and a goal for my students to sign the fish before they leave," said Bain. "It seems ridiculous, but I have found that middle school students love anything goofy or quirky."

Rhythm

Bain requires that all students in the program either purchase a combination tuner/metronome or buy apps for their phone. "I approach the rehearsal like I would my own personal practice," explained Bain. "After an initial long-tone warmup on my saxophone, I use a metronome. I want to instill the same habits in my students."

With beginners, Bain recently implemented a counting system created by Texas middle school band director Darcy Vogt Williams, called *Teaching*

Rhythm Logically. This system provides a logical sequence for teaching subdivision of sustained notes. Students pulse the underlying eighth-note subdivision of whole notes, half notes, and quarter notes with their voice. For example, a whole note is four beats with eight pulses, and a half note is two beats with four pulses. Students count eighth notes "1-tay-2-tay" and count four sixteenth notes "1-ti-tay-tah."

Prior to this, Bain taught the students to shake their hands on the sustained eighth notes for dotted quarter-note rhythms. For example, a quarter note would be "clap-shake" while a dotted quarter note is "clap-shake-shake." "Younger students need to move and feel the tactile-kinesthetic aspects of rhythm," Bain said. "We want them to internalize it before they put the instrument to their face." Bain also teaches students to tap their foot because it helps them feel a steady pulse and provides visual evidence of their internal sense of pulse.

Balance
Bain defines balance as finding the correct dynamic levels, so the audience can hear all musical layers, and the right dynamic levels so that all instruments within each musical layer are equal. "We have to constantly balance the overall ensemble timbre so that we can clearly hear the melody, countermelody, and accompaniment," Bain said. She uses composer and pedagogue Francis McBeth's "pyramid of sound" concept, teaching students that the lowest voices should be strongest, middle voices slightly softer, and higher voices even softer. In the daily warmup, she has students play concert F, building from the lowest voices to the highest and guiding students' ears to inconsistencies. Bain also has students play basic chords such as F major, B-flat major, or E-flat major and then balances them incorrectly, gradually teaching students how to adjust on their own. Bain will also use percentages to balance chords properly. For example, she might ask the third trumpets for 10 percent more of their note and 5 percent less from the second trumpets. "We have to teach students from the very beginning to be aurally aware of what is and what is not correct balance and then constantly adjust in rehearsal," she said.

Musicianship
Bain teaches musicianship through demonstration and modeling. She allows students to choose their preference and then asks them to explain their choices. "To create independent musicians, we have to give students

a variety of approaches and creative options, just like we do when teaching tone quality and ensemble balance," she said. When performing a certain composition, Bain will also have students compare and contrast the musical choices in several recordings of the same piece as well as other pieces by the same composer. This variety provides opportunities to discuss musical ideas, helping students become more conscious of how a crescendo is pushed all the way through to its destination or how breathing occurs at appropriate times within phrases.

Words of Wisdom

When envisioning the goals for each student, each ensemble, and the program as a whole, Bain believes "good is the enemy of great." She said:

> We have to set clear goals and make detailed plans for how we are going to get students from point A to point B without limiting their potential for success. I want students to thoroughly enjoy not only the fun aspects of the band program but also the significant moments that are going to endure through their high school and college careers. Making great music is the number-one priority, and the fun comes with it.

Bain has created a culture in her program where students can expect to have fun and perform with a high level of musicianship, learning principles of hard work, teamwork, and dedication. "You do not have to be a dictator to get students to work hard; you can be the beloved coach," Bain said. "I am very enthusiastic about what I do, and I encourage students to jump right in with me on this adventure."

Erin Cole

"Don't make excuses; work to create solutions."

Erin Cole was the director of bands at Tapp Middle School in Cobb County, Georgia for twenty-two years. She received her bachelor's degree in music education from the University of Georgia.

Program Structure

After one year as an assistant director, Erin Cole became the director of bands at Tapp Middle School in Powder Springs, Georgia. At the time, the surrounding area was rapidly expanding, and band enrollment exceeded six hundred students. Shortly after her promotion, two middle schools were built, alleviating the overcrowded classrooms. In Cole's final year, there were 850 students enrolled in grades six through eight, with 385 students participating in band. The orchestra and choir programs were also active, with more than 85 percent of the school involved in fine arts. Cole attributed this to the value of arts in the community and continued success of the programs. "Parents understood the expectation involved and saw the success of our students," she said. "They wanted their child to be a part of something great."

During Cole's tenure in Cobb County, band began in sixth grade, and students were placed in ensembles according to grade level. Cole and her colleague taught two heterogeneous beginner classes as well as two seventh and two eighth-grade bands, each divided by ability level. Each class met daily for fifty minutes. Through fundraising efforts, a percussion instructor was hired to assist with the concert ensembles and teach the beginning percussion class. Students could also participate in jazz band, which met during the school day and twice a week after school.

The concert bands performed four concerts every year, and all eighth graders performed a special Halloween concert. The top seventh-grade band, top eighth-grade band, and a combined ensemble of the second seventh and eighth-grade bands performed at the district festival in the spring. Most students also auditioned for the district honor band and the Georgia all-state band in the first semester and participated in a solo and ensemble fundraiser concert in the second semester. Cole emphasized the value of these performance opportunities:

> Directors need to find any opportunity they can to get students fired up about playing their instrument, because there is enormous value in motivating them early on. When they prepare for honor band or all-state and make it, they get a taste of success and want to do more. You begin to build your culture when students see the progress other students are making. We had an all-state tuba player who stayed after school every day in sixth grade to practice. We helped him every day, and once he started having success, other students took notice. Looking down the road, this student will most likely get a scholarship to play tuba in college.

Since grade level primarily dictated ensemble placement, the instrumentation and setup fluctuated each year. Cole typically had her flutes in the first row. First and second clarinets sat to her left in the second row, followed by oboes and the remaining flutes. Third clarinets were on the left in the third row, followed by low reeds, alto saxophones, and French horns. "Having the alto saxophones next to the French horns is very helpful at the middle-school level," Cole said. "I would even alternate French horn and alto saxophone players in rehearsal if they had similar parts." Trumpets were seated in the fourth row on the conductor's left, followed by trombones or euphoniums, and tubas were in the fifth row to the conductor's right. Cole attempted to keep all the low voices in the same location, with the low reeds seated directly in front of the trombones or euphoniums.

Additional Instruction

In Cole's final year, Tapp Middle School was a mixed socioeconomic demographic with 68 percent of students on a free-and-reduced lunch program. Many families lacked the necessary funds to enroll in private lessons, so Cole used fundraising dollars to hire instrument-specific teachers for sectionals and master classes and provided scholarships for double-reed students to study privately. Several local teachers with corporate sponsorships, including members of the Atlanta Symphony Orchestra, gave private lessons or sectionals for free. "Our job is to find those kids that will be successful if given the opportunity for private lessons and seek out every resource, program, and financial possibility to help them," she said.

Over time, Cole and her staff developed a culture in which students would come in early or stay after for additional practice and assistance. After school, students could participate in chamber ensembles such as flute choir or percussion ensemble. During the second semester, the top seventh and eighth-grade bands had weekly sectionals. "Early-morning and after-school band was never mandatory," Cole said. "But once students saw their friends participating and being successful, fifty to seventy-five students typically came in each morning or stayed after school for individual help on playing tests, mock auditions, or to have their own sectionals."

Recruitment
Students came to Tapp from two and a half elementary schools. Recruitment efforts began at the end of the first semester, when several chamber ensembles played holiday songs before concerts and events at the various elementary schools. Posters and flyers were displayed, and every fifth grader was given a packet called "Join the Band!" The packet included frequently asked questions, the benefits of joining the band, and other advocacy materials. In the second semester, all fifth graders toured Tapp, and the top seventh-grade band would play current pop or movie tunes.

In the spring, fifth graders interested in joining the band attended an "instrument testing" night. The jazz band performed, and local private lesson teachers, band directors, and advanced college musicians demonstrated each of the instruments and performed recognizable songs. Students were tested and ranked on every instrument. Cole discussed instrument choices with families at the final station and managed the overall instrumentation. She also distributed a list of recommended instruments, provided music store brochures, and promoted lessons over the summer. If parents were concerned about cost, Cole would encourage students to choose school-owned instruments. "It is important for students to play an instrument they are successful on in the testing process, but also that they are excited about playing," she said. "When students are excited about their instrument choice, they tend to be more motivated to practice, and as a result, there will be a successful retention rate in the program."

At the beginning of the school year, Cole made one final presentation to catch sixth-grade students who had not yet signed up. She also was present during the lunch period and in the hallways during class changes to talk with students about joining the band. Each year, Cole modified her recruitment process based on the students and the community. However, she always tried to provide multiple opportunities throughout the year to sign up for band. "Motivation is key," she said. "Encourage all students to at least come to the band room and try the instruments. Some students may not even know they are interested in joining band until they try to play an instrument."

Beginning Band Curriculum
Due to district academic requirements, beginning band students were placed in one of two heterogeneous classes. Cole and her assistant then divided these classes into woodwinds and brass to allow for specific instruction. With combined instrument classes, Cole noted the difficulty of working with individual instruments. However, she used this as an opportunity to teach patience and proper rehearsal etiquette. Cole gave students silent tasks such as music theory packets or she would play informative videos provided by the *Essential Elements* method book.

When Cole first began as the head director, she taught 250 beginners by herself in a school environment where there were minimum expectations for student behavior. "Developing a routine and system of expectation was necessary to have a successful classroom management plan," she said. "Understanding proper classroom behavior was the first task in beginning band." Students entered the classroom silently, and each day, Cole placed a name tag on each chair. The students would be seated and place the name tag on the music stand facing the director. "At the beginning of the year, this was a great way to learn students' names," Cole said. The name tag also acted as a classroom management tool, as students could be moved around if they were disruptive. Likewise, the name tag served as an incentive and "badge of honor" because students would accumulate stickers throughout the year if they earned a perfect score on a playing exam. Once all students were in their assigned chairs, they placed their instruments on the floor, Cole gave announcements, and all students unpacked their materials and assembled their instruments together. Regarding this procedure, she said:

> Many people are shocked and do not believe me when I said I very rarely had behavior problems in my rehearsals. Students did not misbehave because we did the same procedure every day and the students knew what to expect. We were consistent in our expectations through eighth grade, and as a result, we seldom had disruptive students. After their first year, the students realized they were successful and continued to buy into the process.

The week after classes began, Cole's feeder high school hosted a "Saturday Band Carnival" to help beginners get started. Band directors from across the county taught sectionals in the morning, assisting students with instrument assembly, hand position, embouchure placement, sound production, and learning the first notes. Lunch was served, and students played games outside in the afternoon. The day concluded with a "show and tell" concert for the other students and parents.

Cole primarily used the *Essential Elements* method book, but also provided supplementary materials from other method books or created exercises depending on the student's needs. With both beginners and the concert ensembles, approximately 75 percent of rehearsal during the first semester was devoted to fundamental skill training. Cole's routine included breathing exercises while reinforcing posture and embouchure placement, singing, long-tone exercises, scales while reinforcing proper hand position, chorales, and excerpts of the concert music. She also adapted exercises from *Essential Elements* to address difficult concepts found in the concert repertoire. She explained her philosophy on fundamentals:

> Everything about teaching middle school has to do with pacing. Spending this long on fundamentals required a variety of creative approaches and multiple ways of presenting the same material. Change the dynamics, articulations, or transpose the exercises to keep students engaged.

Woodwinds, brass, and percussion rehearsed separately most of the time. Cole and her colleagues were always in communication about the progress of each ensemble and the goals for the subsequent rehearsals. "We were always planning for the next rehearsal, the next concert, the next year, with the goal in mind and working backward from there," she added.

Repertoire Selection

When choosing repertoire, Cole continually assessed where students were in their development and where they needed to be by the end of the year. She searched for quality works that highlighted the strengths of the ensemble while attending to the various weaknesses. Cole said:

> Many times, I hear an ensemble play a piece with exposed passages for the weakest sections or solos for the weakest players. In the end, this is not a positive experience for the child, the ensemble, or the audience. Directors have to know the ensemble and where they can get them in a two- or three-month period. If you choose music that is too difficult, you are skipping steps in the process, which later becomes a detriment.

The repertoire Cole chose reinforced concepts addressed in the fundamentals or the method book. For example, when the method book introduced a compound rhythm, she often chose a composition with a compound time signature. Each concert always included an easier lyrical work that allowed students to improve their aural awareness and explore musical phrasing without the technical distraction. Most importantly, Cole tried to choose music that the students were excited about practicing on their own and rehearsing daily for an extended period.

Tone

For Cole, producing a characteristic tone quality was not negotiable. "If we do not properly address the quality of sound from the very beginning, every other musical element suffers," she said. Once she established a routine for entering the classroom, students learned proper posture and hand position. Cole introduced breathing exercises to reinforce these concepts and often used balloons as a visualizer. "Balloons allow the student to see if they are moving air or not," remarked Cole. "They would breathe in for four counts and out for four, in for two and out for eight, or any other combination of counts, and students were always told to use all of the counts to fill up the balloon and never have leftover air."

Establishing a correct embouchure and producing a characteristic sound on the mouthpiece or head joint was the next goal. Students buzzed or played familiar songs and sometimes created original melodies. "These could be as simple as high and low sounds, but the goal was to sound the correct pitch with correct embouchure," said Cole. Brass players mimicked the sound of sirens and also worked on play-along exercises developed by famed trumpeter James Thompson. The first playing exam was a mouthpiece test in which students had to sustain specific pitches and/or buzz a simple song.

Once students could achieve a quality tone on the mouthpiece and transfer it to the instrument, Cole would begin extending their range through Remington exercises and scales. In her experience as a clinician, she has witnessed many directors who fail to teach the students how to make quality sounds in lower and upper registers of the instrument. She said:

> Many bands will play pieces that have extended ranges for the woodwinds and brass but never play, on a regular basis, fundamental exercises, scales, or melodies in the method book that teach students how to do that correctly. Range-building exercises have to continue through eighth grade if you want to play challenging repertoire.

Cole believes that students need to hear quality sounds every day to make quality sounds every day. She provided students with recordings and videos of professional musicians to improve their aural awareness and understand the long-term goal. She also constantly modeled on the instruments and believes it is essential that middle school directors learn to play the instruments they teach. "My college methods classes only taught me how to play the instruments at a basic level, not how to teach others to play the instruments," Cole said. "Therefore, I spent a lot of time early on in my career learning the intricacies of every instrument, so I felt comfortable teaching and modeling for my students."

Intonation
When introducing intonation, Cole stressed the importance of performing on quality instruments and forming the correct embouchure. "If the student sets the embouchure correctly and they are breathing properly, the general intonation in the middle range should be decent," she said. Cole frequently demonstrated and had students model good intonation versus bad intonation, using sound waves to guide their ears. Students would use tuners to learn about instrument tendencies and inconsistencies. Then, as

they developed, the tuners became a guide, with more importance placed on adjusting to the ensemble. Cole repeatedly asked questions in rehearsal about what students heard and how to fix it, so they could ultimately take responsibility for their intonation. Her body language also taught students what was correct and incorrect. "If I made a face or cringed, that was always a sign to the students that it is not good," remarked Cole. "Over time, they learned to gauge for themselves what was appropriate and would also start to cringe!"

Technique

Cole used scales daily to develop technical skill. Students would say the note names at specific tempo with correct fingerings or positions. "Forming the correct hand position from the start and reminding students to keep their fingers close to the keys at all times is crucial," she said. The beginning woodwind class learned the concert A-flat major first because it not only correlated with the method book, but the clarinets did not have to cross the break. When Cole introduced the concert B-flat major, E-flat major, and F major scales, the flutes and saxophones would join the brass class so she could work on crossing the break with the clarinets. More scales were then added, typically to correlate with the method book or needs of the repertoire.

To encourage individual practice and technical development, Cole had a karate-inspired incentive system. Students earned colored stickers if they successfully completed a pass-off that corresponded to the curriculum. For example, a student earned a yellow sticker if they could play their concert A-flat major scale and a specific line out of the method book. A student then earned a red sticker if they could play their concert B-flat major scale along with two lines out of the method book.

Cole also played "band baseball" on Fridays after a playing assessment. Three chairs were lined up in the front of the room to resemble bases. Cole split the class into two teams and assigned a team captain, and the students named their teams. A student from one team would play an assigned line out of the method book, and if they played it correctly, they sat in the first chair. If they played it with mistakes, the team earned an out. If the next student played the line correctly, that student sat in the first chair and the first student moved to the second chair. Students on the team continued playing, moving chairs and earning runs by reaching "home," stopping when they earned three outs. Cole would have students perform more challenging lines for homeruns or grand slams. "I chose what lines I wanted them to play," she said. "Not only is it fun for the students, but it's also a great way to hear students individually and also hold them more accountable."

Rhythm

Before teaching a counting system, Cole taught students to recognize note values. Students would clap on the downbeat of a whole note and say "Whole-note-three-four" on each beat. Half notes would be chanted "half-note" on each beat to emphasize the subdivision. Students would then attach numbers to the note values. When introducing new rhythms, Cole would write the rhythm on the board while students wrote it out themselves. She often had a "rhythm of the day" in which students would write one or two measures using specific rhythmic parameters. Cole would write one or two student compositions on the board, and the student who composed it would have to write in the counts. The class would then say the rhythm, clap it, and sizzle it. A metronome was always used to instill a steady pulse; it also acted as a classroom management tool, allowing Cole to move around the classroom to fix hand positions or posture and keep students on task.

When students were preparing for honor band or all-state band auditions, Cole used *Sight-Reading Factory* to develop individual sight-reading skills. On this subscription-based website, students can select their instrument, difficulty, key signature, time signature, and length. They can then record themselves playing the exercise and compare it to the correct version. When teaching sight-reading to the full ensemble, Cole was fortunate to have a classroom set of several method books in her library. These included *101 Rhythmic Rest Patterns*, *Band Techniques Step-by-Step*, *Tone Studies*, *Essential Technique*, and *Strictly Technique*. She also had a set of folders with past music from the district sight-reading contest. Books or folders would be distributed, and Cole would give a detailed explanation of the sight-reading process and procedure. She said:

> Middle school students must practice this process several times throughout the year. At first, make it as easy as a line out of the method book to build their confidence and their understanding. Then, they have the tools and skill when they have to sight-read at a contest or festival.

Balance and Blend

Since the beginning band classes split between woodwinds, brass, and percussion, students did not hear some of the instruments until the first full ensemble rehearsal. Therefore, Cole was adamant about setting the expectation for appropriate behavior before the first full ensemble rehearsal. She said:

> Students need to be prepared in advance for what is going to happen. For example, clarinets will squeak, odd sounds will occur, and students will get distracted. They are so excited and will want to play loudly because the sound environment has changed. Directors need to continually remind students to play the same volume they do every day.

Cole would have each section play so that students could see where the instruments were and hear how they sounded. She then explained how ensemble sound should be prioritized using Francis McBeth's "pyramid of sound" concept; the low instruments played a concert F or B-flat, then middle voices, and then upper voices with specific feedback given to adjust. Once students understood the basics, Cole would introduce the concepts of blend and timbre by having different combinations of instruments play together.

With varied instrumentations and ability levels at the middle school level, Cole frequently edited parts to fix balance issues and create more clarity. She said:

> You have to be open to adjusting some parts to the ensemble. Rewrite parts for instruments that are not present in the ensemble, place more students on second or third parts if the balance is too bright, or change the dynamics to achieve more clarity. Respond to the issue and do whatever you have to do to make them sound good without ruining the integrity of the piece or what the composer intended.

Musicianship

Cole believes in having all of the concert ensembles, including beginners, perform a lyrical work on every concert. "The earlier you introduce musicianship, the more it will develop," she said. "Lyrical pieces are the best way to teach students how to shape music and create longer phrases over an extended period." Chorales were part of the daily fundamentals to address these conceptual issues at the simplest level. Cole said:

We would play the first four measures or first line and then talk about where the music is going and why. We talked about and practiced where we needed to breathe and not breathe to make that happen. Even with beginners, we cannot forget to talk about how to make music with them.

Cole would also play recordings of professional ensembles to provide an aural model and reinforce musical concepts. She often used analogies to relate subjective musical concepts to everyday life. "We have to remember that these are middle school students who have limited life experience," Cole said. "The challenge is to find what is relevant in their world and ways we can connect these ideas to their interests and their culture."

Words of Wisdom

Cole encourages directors to create long-term and short-term goals for their program and focus on solving problems rather than making excuses. Cole and her students encountered many challenging circumstances, but that did not inhibit them from achieving excellence and performing at a high level. She focused on building a consistent routine, teaching music rather than addressing behavior problems, being as genuine as possible, and creating a safe environment and positive experience for every student.

> Get to know your students and be genuine because kids can instantly tell if you care about them or not. Know their names, ask how their day is going, and talk about something they are interested in other than band, because, in return, they will trust you completely. When parents see this, they will buy into your program and word will spread throughout the community.

It was never Cole's intention to teach middle school for her entire career. However, once she witnessed the enormous progress made from sixth to eighth grade, from knowing nothing to watching them grow through high school, she could not imagine herself doing anything else. "The progress is remarkable and extremely rewarding," Cole said. "There is never a dull moment, and there is always a story—or five—every single day."

Chip De Stefano

"Students are a reflection of their teacher."

Chip De Stefano has been the director of bands at Oliver McCracken Middle School in Skokie, Illinois since 1996. He holds a bachelor's degree in trombone performance and a master's degree in music education from Northwestern University.

Program Structure

Oliver McCracken Middle School is a small, racially diverse school of 375 students in grades six through eight, located in the northern suburbs of Chicago. Over forty languages are spoken, and, for many students, English is a second language. McCracken is part of Skokie School District 73.5, which also includes Elizabeth Meyer Primary School and John Middleton Elementary School. Students from McCracken and seven other elementary school districts attend Niles Township High Schools, a separate school district consisting of a different administration and school board. De Stefano student-taught at McCracken and became the director of bands when his mentor teacher retired at the end of the year.

Band begins in fourth grade at John Middleton Elementary School, and for the first two years, students are pulled from their academic classes once a week for thirty-minute group lessons. The time changes each week so that students do not consistently miss the same class. Fourth graders meet as a full ensemble once a week, after school, for forty-five minutes. Fifth graders rehearse after school twice a week for forty-five minutes.

Pull-out lessons and sectionals continue at the middle school, with the full ensembles meeting before and after school. The top ensemble, symphonic band, meets before school for thirty-three minutes every day except Wednesdays. It also meets on Tuesdays after school for ninety minutes. The second band, concert band, meets before school on Tuesdays and Thursdays for thirty-three minutes and after school on Tuesdays for one hour. De Stefano's part-time assistant, a retired high school band director, leads those rehearsals. This structure has evolved since De Stefano started, and the administration, faculty, and community continue to be supportive and flexible with the schedule.

The symphonic band performs several concerts throughout the school year. The first is a recruitment concert at the elementary school in early October. They also perform a fall concert in October, a winter concert in December, a pre-contest performance in March, at district contest in March, at state contest in April, at the Illinois SuperState Festival in early May, and at a mass concert with all of the bands at the end of May. There are also periodic performances at the primary school for preschoolers and kindergartners, and special events as invited.

In October, students can audition for a district band hosted by the Illinois Music Education Association. They have to prepare a two-octave chromatic scale (three octaves for clarinet), seven major scales and the relative melodic minor scale, an etude out of the *Second Book of Practical Studies* series published by Belwin, and the first parts from the concert repertoire. This material is also used to determine chair placements in symphonic band at the beginning of the year. In February, students are encouraged to audition for the All-Illinois Junior Band, a statewide honor ensemble De Stefano co-founded. Students prepare a two-octave chromatic scale and two etudes out of the *Supplemental Studies* method book, published by Rubank.

Every February, all sixth, seventh, and eighth graders are required to play a solo at a contest organized by the Illinois Grade School Music Association. Students can also elect to do ensembles on their own, in addition to their solo. Fifth graders who are studying privately have the option of participating in the solo contest. A week before the event, De Stefano holds a mock contest. He hires local band directors and instructors to provide feedback, and the students get to perform for their peers and families.

Private Lessons

Although students meet for sectionals and private lessons during the day, they are encouraged to take lessons with local instructors and area professionals. "I never require private lessons but recommend them heavily," De Stefano said. "We try to push lessons from the very beginning, even if the child has just started, and especially if the child shows potential." He keeps a list of recommended teachers who teach well at the middle school level and have a similar pedagogical approach to his own.

Ensemble Setup

De Stefano organizes his rehearsal room with ample space to move around. With beginners, he will set up the chairs in groups of two so that every student is accessible. He said:

> Don't underestimate the importance of the way you set up your ensemble as a tool to help students get better. When I teach, I am rarely on the podium conducting; I am on what I call my "moving" podium. Moving around makes it easy to correct posture, hand position, and embouchures while the band is playing.

De Stefano places any sixth, seventh, or eighth-grade student in the top ensemble if they can handle the responsibility and rigor. Therefore, the symphonic band typically has more students than the concert band. His ideal instrumentation is eight flutes, two oboes, nine to twelve clarinets, two bass clarinets, four alto saxophones, two tenor saxophones, two baritone saxophones, one or two bassoons, eight trumpets, four horns, six trombones, two euphoniums, three tubas, and six percussionists. However, numbers fluctuate every year.

De Stefano models his seating arrangement after composer and band director Doug Akey. The French horns sit in the center of the front row, with the saxophones directly behind them. This location makes it easier for the horns to hear their parts and be heard in the overall ensemble sound. Placement of the other instruments is dependent on the music and the students. De Stefano added:

> Students learn a lot from each other, and advanced students can pull along the weaker ones. In some cases, I might move the two extremes to sit next to each other so that the stronger student can be a positive role model throughout the rehearsal.

Recruitment

In October, De Stefano gives a presentation about joining the band to all fourth-grade general music classes. He highlights the experiences the students will have in band, outlines the expectations, and shares photos, videos, and recordings. He also introduces the instrument options. A few days later, the symphonic band performs for the entire elementary school, with each section leader demonstrating and performing a recognizable melody on his or her instrument. Shortly thereafter, each fourth grader, regardless of whether they will join band or not, samples two instruments and chooses the instrument on which they were the most successful. De Stefano typically has sixty to seventy beginners each year, and students can start in fifth grade if space is available. He starts all of the instruments, and because progress is slow in the first two years, students are not limited physically by instrument choice. He said:

> If a clarinet player cannot cover all of the tone holes or a trombone player cannot reach seventh position, we do not let that stop them from choosing that instrument. We move at a pace that is both physically and mentally comfortable for them to be successful, knowing that we have two years and they will grow in the process.

Retention

"My only goal for the fourth and fifth graders is that they sign up to play the next year," De Stefano said. Over the course of the year, he tries to maintain their initial excitement by building intrinsic motivation through individual practice and performances. "It is obvious, but students who practice are more likely to be successful, and students who are successful are more likely to sign up again," De Stefano said. "Therefore, we have to teach our students the value of practicing and how to do it effectively."

De Stefano's philosophy of motivation and student practice is rooted in Abraham Maslow's Hierarchy of Needs. He said:

> Maslow states that individuals are motivated because they must satisfy specific needs: physiological, safety, belonging, self-esteem, and self-actualization. Ideally, we want students to practice because they are motivated to become the best musicians that they can be and because they want the band to be successful. However, if we look at the typical ways directors

motivate kids to practice, they do not motivate in this manner. They use grades (esteem), chair placement (esteem, belonging, safety), playing tests (esteem), challenges (safety), fear (safety), intimidation (esteem, safety), guilt (belonging), or superficial rewards (physiological). While these methods can work with some students, they only meet the lower needs. We must get our students to take ownership of their learning to reach self-actualization.

Students do not receive grades for band nor does De Stefano require practice charts. Instead, students set personal and ensemble goals at the beginning of the year. De Stefano conducts playing tests throughout the rehearsal process, and students assess their own progress while De Stefano provides additional commentary. "I want them to take responsibility for their successes and failures," he said. "Failures are okay as long as students learn from them. They provide the opportunity to talk about how to get better by practicing."

Once a student understands why to practice, De Stefano teaches them how to practice. He provides a step-by-step guide for beginners that outlines the five W's of practice:

- Who? You, the student.
- When? The same time each day.
- Where? A quiet, well-lit room that is free from distractions and has a straight-back chair and music stand.
- Why? It is the only way you will get better.
- What? Specific excerpts or exercises focusing on every aspect of performance (tone, rhythm, range, scales, sight-reading, articulation, and dynamics).

De Stefano runs a mentorship program to assist beginners who are struggling and motivate older students. He said:

This program is a fantastic way to help a struggling student, a student who just switched instruments, or a student who needs extra help. The mentee receives guidance from a trusted student who is close in age, understands the expectations, and performs at a high level. Mentors provide an excellent model that the mentee can aspire to achieve while getting valuable, real-world teaching experience.

In addition to practicing, De Stefano builds motivation through performances and by giving students a long-term vision for being a musician. "One of the few things that matches the initial excitement of opening the case for the first time is the excitement students feel as their first performance approaches," he said. "The sooner they are ready for the first performance, the better." The first concert with the beginners is paired with the symphonic band. This allows beginning students and parents to see the progress made over four years and, for the finale, there is a joint performance of the "Mickey Mouse March." De Stefano invites guest performers and local professionals to play for the students and will post flyers for community or university band concerts in the area. "Even if they do not actively go, they know groups like the Northshore Concert Band exist and that there are opportunities to continue playing through college and into adulthood," he said.

Beginning Band Curriculum

At the first group lesson, De Stefano distributes a detailed handout for each instrument that students can use while practicing at home. Posture is reinforced with the phrase, "Sit tall, feet flat, fanny front." Next, there is a step-by-step guide to forming a proper embouchure, and it is De Stefano's goal to set them up correctly the first time so they can make a sound. "Otherwise, if they cannot make a sound, they will go home and try by any means necessary," he said. Students play a series of head joint or mouthpiece exercises, followed by breathing and sizzling exercises. The handout also includes an explanation of how to put the instrument together and how to play the first notes. Students gradually add more notes and begin learning scales with each successive lesson. De Stefano uses the *Standard of Excellence* method book with beginners, and by the end of the first year, most fourth graders can play through page 15.

In fifth grade, De Stefano restarts every student from the beginning to reinforce fundamental concepts. However, they often use a different method book that moves at a quicker pace to fill in any learning gaps. "It helps those kids who did not practice over the summer to ease back into it with minimum frustration," he said. He also includes supplemental exercises such as lip and register slurs, rhythm and articulation exercises, and extended scales.

Repertoire Selection

When choosing repertoire, De Stefano referenced teacher and composer Douglas Akey, who said, "If the musical difficulty meets or exceeds the technical difficulty, then it is probably a piece worthy of being played." De Stefano added, "The music should be tuneful, have equitable difficulty in all the parts, and the technique should not get in the way of the music." De Stefano tries to find music that does not necessarily teach concepts such as compound meter or key signatures but that extends the student's musical knowledge. He rarely plays new music unless the musical quality is equal to or surpasses the standard band literature. He said:

> We cannot forget the classics. Many directors are looking for the next "English Folk Song Suite" instead of performing "English Folk Song Suite." Performing only one movement of many of these standard works may make them more accessible.

The symphonic band will play twenty to thirty works each year. For the fall recruitment concert, five or six works, including "The Star-Spangled Banner," are performed. These are mostly grade-2 compositions, possibly grade-3 or even grade-4. "With the harder pieces, we might only play the first thirty measures and continue to work on it for the winter concert," De Stefano said. "We also do not always perform everything we rehearse." If De Stefano knows he is going to play a particular composition in May, he might program an easier work by the same composer on the fall or winter concert. "I try to program for our weaknesses in the fall and program for our strengths in the spring," he said.

Score Study and Rehearsal Preparation

De Stefano conducts the wind ensemble at the University of Chicago, in addition to his responsibilities at McCracken. He finds the planning process to be drastically different between the two ensembles. At the University of Chicago, De Stefano develops a strong mental image of what he wants the music to sound like and understands each element of the score prior to rehearsal. While it is a similar process at McCracken, planning for rehearsals is dependent on the time of year and progress of the students. He records his rehearsals and listens to them while watching the score, creating a plan for the next several rehearsals. The symphonic band rehearses for thirty-three minutes, and at the beginning of the year, De Stefano may easily spend twenty minutes on fundamentals. "The goal is to master those exercises early in the year and reinforce them later as we apply the concepts to the repertoire," he said. De Stefano primarily focuses on ensemble issues such as balance, blend, timbre, and cross-sections of the music during rehearsals. Sectionals are then focused exclusively on the music and technical development through the music.

Tone

Pedagogically, De Stefano prioritizes tone quality above all other skills. By the end of the first year, his goal is for every student to produce a characteristic tone on their instrument. To do so, the student needs a quality instrument in proper working condition. De Stefano distributes a list of recommended equipment when students sign up for band class and will encourage step-up brands as they progress through the program. With beginners, De Stefano believes students need an aural model of the goal, saying, "Kids are not able to produce a good sound unless they know what a good sound sounds like." He develops this aural image through guided listening exercises of professional players and ensembles. De Stefano will ask students to describe the difference between two recordings. "Having the students come up with descriptive words has more meaning, because the students have a personalized aural concept of the goal," he said. Additionally, De Stefano never provides a model for his students that is less than outstanding and discourages directors from playing secondary instruments in which they lack proficiency. "If we want our students' standards to be high, then excellence needs to be the norm," he said. "If they hear their teacher playing with a stuffy clarinet sound, that is the sound they will try to model."

Rehearsals begin with breathing exercises to develop proper breath support. Students stand to reinforce proper posture and place their hands behind their head, so they are able to take a full breath more easily. Students breathe in for eight counts and out for eight counts, in for four counts and out for four counts, in for two counts and out for two counts, and in for one count and out for eight counts. They repeat each sequence four times. Students then sizzle to add resistance and practice using air efficiently to sustain long phrases. They then transfer these exercises to their instruments, where they blow "warm" air, except for the saxophones, who blow "cold" air.

Developing a proper embouchure is the next step to producing a character-istic tone quality. Students play glissando patterns, echo patterns, and long tones on their mouthpieces or head joints to strengthen their embouchure, increase lip flexibility, and develop ear-training skills. All students then play lip slurs or register slurs, long tones, slow scales, and homophonic chorales. De Stefano said:

> Perhaps the most significant challenge for young students is sustained playing. We use homophonic chorales to develop this skill. Each instrument has the soprano, alto, tenor, and bass line so that everyone can be actively involved in the rehearsal. We sing through each line on the syllable "da" because it most closely applies to the articulation they should be using. If groups are reluctant to sing, it is equally effective if the students first say the line on "da." We then play through the chorale without articulating any note. The reason kids do not play sustained is that they tend to stop the air between notes. What we need is for the air to be constant, with the tongue lightly breaking the air for each attack. Performing without the use of the tongue allows the students to understand how the air should move. We then add a light articulation, making sure the air continues to move.

Intonation

"Good tone can mask intonation problems, and if the student has a decent instrument, proper embouchure, and air support, then intonation problems should be minimal," De Stefano said. Beginners learn to hear each note in their heads exactly how they want it to sound by first humming individual notes and eventually singing solfege patterns. De Stefano guides the students' ears to listen to their neighbor and not themselves, and to distinguish between pitches that are in tune and out of tune. He introduces the concept of "beats" or "waves" by having two students play the same note on the same instrument. De Stefano makes the difference more noticeable by adjusting one of the instruments to be drastically out of tune. Once the students recognize the waves, they each play individually with a drone and other students determine who sounds higher. De Stefano adjusts that student's instrument even if he knows the answer is wrong. The student plays with the drone again, and De Stefano asks if the speed of the waves has increased, decreased, or disappeared. De Stefano explains that if the waves speed up, they should quickly adjust the other way. The process continues until the two instruments are in tune with each other and with the drone. De Stefano added:

> Nothing kills a rehearsal like going down the row and telling students what and how much to adjust. We need to put the responsibility on the students, so they can adjust on their own when intonation issues arise. It is important to emphasize from the beginning that the only real error is to not adjust at all.

In fifth and sixth grade, students delve deeper into intonation skills. They use tuners to learn which notes are consistently sharp or flat on their instruments. Students learn how to adjust the pitch higher and lower through embouchure tension, amount of mouthpiece or reed, air temperature, alternate fingerings, shading, and venting.

When tuning chords, De Stefano uses a specific order to make it easier for students to hear how their note fits within the chord and to know what adjustments they need to make for the chord to be in tune with itself. He begins by tuning the root (typically in the tubas and low reeds) followed by others who have the tonic. Next, he tunes the fifth, then the third, followed by the seventh, and finally any other chord extensions. In this process, De Stefano believes specific, detailed comments are essential. He explained:

> Let students know where they should be listening to match pitch. Usually, we want them listening down. If something is in octaves, the upper octave should tune to the lower octave. Addressing specific sections, specific notes, their role and tuning tendency in the chord, and precisely where they should be listening, is how we create clarity.

Technique

For De Stefano, proper hand position is essential to the development of technique. He teaches students that the fingers must remain close to the keys and move like machines. Likewise, beginners are taught that motor memory and tempo are mutually exclusive. He further explained:

> If there is a technical issue, I try to differentiate between dexterity and evenness. If the student's fingers are not moving fast enough, then we start the excerpt at a slow tempo and gradually increase it with every repetition. However, if the student has developed the technical facility and the issue is

evenness, we will review the excerpt at a slow tempo, five to ten times, and then immediately play it at tempo. If the issue is with the evenness of the technique, gradually increasing the tempo increases the chance of introducing small errors in the muscle memory. Playing it slowly several times allows it to feel automatic to the student, and the technique easily transfers when the excerpt is played faster.

Other strategies De Stefano uses for developing coordination and facility in a method book exercise or technically difficult passage include: saying the note names, saying the note names while fingering along, sizzling the rhythm while fingering, buzzing while fingering, and singing the melody while fingering. Students will also play every other measure or every other note, play the melody backward, subdivide the melody into eighth or sixteenth notes, alter the rhythmic pattern, add different dynamics or articulations, or play to an accompaniment track. The variety stimulates student engagement and allows De Stefano to provide detailed feedback on tone, articulation, and vertical alignment in each repetition.

Rhythm

De Stefano believes middle school band students must develop an inner sense of pulse and a vocabulary of rhythms, so they are able to perform new rhythms without assistance. He uses *Teaching Rhythm Logically* by Darcy Vogt Williams, and students are taught their counting system from their very first rehearsal. They progress through a series of rhythm charts throughout the year. "Particularly in the first two years of instruction, students are counting and working on rhythm patterns that are more challenging than the rhythmic demands in the repertoire," said De Stefano. With any fundamental exercise or difficult rhythmic passage, students will count the particular passage with a metronome, sometimes at a slower tempo. De Stefano will have the students play the part subdivided into eighth notes or sixteenth notes. They also write in their music where the releases should occur. De Stefano spends considerable time discussing releases with beginners, so they understand that the beats happen between the counts. He said:

If there is a dotted half note followed by a quarter rest and the students count "1, 2, 3" and release on 3, then they have only held the note for two full beats. They must release the note on count 4 to hold the dotted half note for full value.

Balance and Blend

As with intonation, De Stefano believes ensemble clarity is achieved by guiding students' listening and providing specific feedback. He uses Francis McBeth's "pyramid of sound" concept because it provides a simple model for understanding balance, although it is not always applicable to concert music. He said:

> I teach students that the "pyramid of sound" concept applies to not only the full ensemble, but also individual sections. If all three clarinet parts are playing, the third clarinets should be the strongest, followed by the seconds and then the firsts. If the flute part is split, the second flutes should play stronger than the first flutes. Additionally, each melodic priority should be a pyramid. The melody should be the strongest voice, followed by the countermelody, and harmonic accompaniment. Even those melodic priorities have smaller pyramids if, for example, the accompaniment is in octaves; the lower octave should always be stronger. Guiding students' listening towards these tiny pyramids helps create ensemble balance, clarity, and greater transparency.

De Stefano also encourages directors to rewrite and rescore the music for better balance and clarity. "Very few bands have ideal instrumentation, especially in small school and middle school programs," De Stefano said. "I typically rewrite or rescore parts if the sections are weaker or missing or if I do not have the correct soloists." When choosing appropriate substitutions, De Stefano retains the essential musical lines and does not compromise the musical content of the piece. He said:

> Always choose a substitute that can play the line in the same range as the original instrument, and try to avoid changing octaves. Whenever possible, choose substitute instruments that have a similar color as the original instrument. For example, substitute one reed instrument for another or one brass instrument for another. Lastly, try to substitute instruments that have the same general musical characteristics as the original instrument, such as timbre and vibrato. This quality is especially important when making substitutions for soloists.

Musicianship

"In order for students to play musically and with style, they need to first understand and master articulation," De Stefano said. The first articulation exercise students learn is a whole note followed by four quarter notes on the first five notes of a B-flat scale. The goal is to keep the air moving from the whole note into the articulated notes. In the next exercise, two eighth notes replace one quarter note and the eighth notes are on different beats in each measure. De Stefano adds staccatos, accents, and legato markings in the third exercise. Students also alternate between concert F and concert E-flat on quarter notes to build simultaneous coordination between the fingers and tongue. As the ensemble progresses through the method book, De Stefano will add articulations and style markings or incorporate them into the daily fundamentals.

One of De Stefano's favorite concepts when teaching musicianship is called "volume painting." He instructs students to add a crescendo as the phrase rises, add a decrescendo as the phrase falls, and always provide direction towards long notes and repeated pitches. "While not always applicable, this is a great default for beginning students," said De Stefano. He also uses the metaphor of an EKG machine to address musical shape and direction. "If the EKG flat-lines, it is a terrible sign. By the same token, if the music flat-lines, there is no life to it either."

Overall, De Stefano believes a student's ability to play musically is the director's responsibility. "We must be great musicians ourselves and be able to show that to our students," he said. "If the director takes a musical approach, it will be evident in the student's performance."

Words of Wisdom
De Stefano sets very high standards for himself as a musician and as a teacher, firmly believing that students will only work or practice as much as he works or practices himself. "Students are a reflection of their teacher," he said. "If I want them to strive to be a great musician and continue learning, I have to do it myself." He encourages directors to find band programs to emulate, find mentors to ask questions of, perform quality music, attend concerts and conventions, and create goals for their program and their students. He said:

> The majority of our time as band directors is spent trying to balance the long-term and short-term goals for our students and our program. However, we only feel the most significant differences after many weeks, months, and years of consistent progress. Focus on the long-term issues and, in the process, we make the short-term goals easier to achieve.

Cheryl Floyd

"Teach the young with only the very best."

Cheryl Floyd retired in May 2017 after thirty-five years as a middle school band director and music educator. She is a graduate of Baylor University.

Program Structure

Cheryl Floyd began her teaching career at St. Mary's Episcopal Day School in Tampa, Florida, where she taught kindergarten through eighth grade. After eighteen months, Floyd moved back to Texas and became the director of bands at Murchison Middle School in Austin Independent School District (ISD). After eight years, Floyd became director of bands at Hill Country Middle School in Eanes ISD and remained there for twenty-five years. When she arrived at Hill Country, Floyd was the fourth band director in two years. "There was a lack of trust from the students and consistency in their skills when I started," Floyd said. "My priority was to show the students, parents, and administration that I cared and had a long-term vision for the program."

Hill Country Middle School had 1,100 students enrolled in grades six through eight, with 225 students participating in band when Floyd retired in 2017. She taught the beginning woodwind classes, assisted with the concert band, and was the primary teacher for the symphonic band. Her assistant taught the beginning brass and percussion classes, was the primary teacher for the concert band, and assisted with the symphonic band. Each class was fifty-two minutes long.

The two concert bands performed seven concerts each year: a fall, winter, and spring concert, plus a Veterans Day program and performances at
pre-contest, region contest, and at a local performance festival. They also
played at two pep rallies and with the high school band at a high school
football game. Additionally, advanced students in the symphonic band
performed with the full orchestra throughout the year.

Floyd taught sectionals year-round, before and after school, for students
in the symphonic band. She explained how sectionals helped her students
develop fundamental skills:

> We have to continue to be responsible for developing fundamentals after
> the first year. We have to extend the range, refine their tone quality, build
> the technique, and improve their rhythmic reading ability. In sectionals,
> we also introduced new music, which allowed me to address instrument-
> specific challenges, assess individual problems, and possibly modify
> the part by simplifying the register, rhythm, technique. Since they were
> homogenous classes, it was also easy to complete graded performance
> assessments.

In the first semester, sectionals focused on mastering eight major scales and
three etudes in preparation for the all-region audition. Once students sub-
mitted these as a recording assignment through Google Classroom, they
learned the last four major scales and other standard etudes. "We rarely
taught the repertoire for the fall and winter concert in sectionals," Floyd
said. "Our goal was to continue developing the individual player through
fundamental exercises and etudes." In April, all students participated in a
solo and ensemble festival. Students in the symphonic band performed a
solo and with an ensemble, students in the concert band performed either
a solo or with an ensemble, and sixth-grade students performed duets and
class solos.

Floyd was fortunate to have many students enrolled in private lessons.
However, it took time to develop that culture. She said:

> We were lucky to be close to the University to Texas. When I first started,
> I brought in professional musicians or graduate students to teach master
> classes. Master classes helped foster a relationship between the student
> and private teacher. If there was a talented student in the class, the private

teacher recruited the student for lessons, and once that student achieved a higher level of success, their peers wanted to enroll. From there, the culture began to grow. If individual students are not able to afford lessons, the master class still provides instrument-specific instruction. However, boosters can provide scholarship assistance, on-campus parent organizations such as PTA have grant money, local businesses might donate money, and principals typically have funds set aside to help students. It never hurts to ask!

Instrumentation

Students recorded their major scales and two etudes as part of their ensemble-placement audition. Although the two concert bands were ability-based, Floyd attempted to split the instrumentation evenly, believing that both ensembles should have complete instrumentation if they were going to receive an evaluation at the region contest. In general, the concert band consisted mostly of seventh graders, and the symphonic band was mostly eighth graders. "Our goal was to have as many eighth graders as possible in the top ensemble so they were prepared and could continue to grow in the high school band," Floyd said. "However, they had to complete the recording assignment and demonstrate the necessary musical skills and maturity to be successful."

When Floyd conducts honors bands, she determines the setup based on the needs of the music, the strengths and weaknesses of each section, and the logistics of the rehearsal and performance space. She typically places the flutes in two rows to her right. "If the flutes are on my right, it allows those students to play louder, which they need to do at the middle school level, and does not affect the overall ensemble balance." For the same reason, the French horns sit to her right with their bells facing into the ensemble. The saxophones often sit behind the French horns to help to provide a pitch reference. At Hill Country, Floyd did not use risers because of practical, logistical, and safety concerns. "We never could count on having risers at the performance venue, and I found that I had more flexibility to change the setup between each concert or between each piece if I did not use them."

Recruitment

Eanes ISD currently consists of six elementary schools, two middle schools, and one high school. During Floyd's tenure, the band directors from the entire cluster worked as a unified team to create a successful recruitment process. In the second semester, fifth graders visited the middle school, and the beginning band, orchestra, and choir would each perform for ten minutes. Floyd demonstrated the instruments and the beginning band played "Crown Point March" by Bruce Pearson, "Chant for Percussion" by Andrew Balent, and "Smoke on the Water" by Deep Purple and arranged by Paul Murtha. A few days later, there was a meet-and-greet at the high school for all fifth graders interested in the band program. The parents met with the middle school and high school directors and discussed the expectations and policies of the program, how conflicts with academics and sports were handled, and addressed any other concerns. At the same time, the high school band students demonstrated the instruments to the fifth graders. The fifth graders chose three or four instruments that piqued their interest, and the directors encouraged them to explore those instruments by listening to performances online.

Following the meet-and-greet, one Saturday was devoted to "instrument interviews" at the high school. There were one or two tables for each instrument, and students were directed to the three or four instruments on their list. The directors assessed physical characteristics such as the size of the student's hands, whether they were double-jointed, and whether they could create the correct embouchure for the instrument. "The high school band director would tell parents that we were looking more than we were listening," Floyd said. Following each interview, the director provided a numerical score between 1 and 5; a score of 1 indicated the instrument was not the right fit and 5 indicated the instrument was ideal for the student. Unless their score was a 1 or 2, students were typically allowed to play their first choice of instrument. Floyd did not start students on tuba until she could assess their ability on trombone or euphonium. Similarly, Floyd considered oboe, bassoon, saxophone, and percussion "specialized" instruments, and she used a more elaborate, double-digit rubric at the interview. Students interested in these instruments were required to choose a second option.

Once the student completed the interview process, the parents could purchase the instrument or set up their rental contract with a local music company. Floyd also distributed a detailed supply list of equipment and accessories for every instrument. She valued parental involvement at this event, saying:

It was great for the parents to be there to see and hear what their child sounded like on specific instruments. Every year, I had to stress the importance of balancing the instrumentation because every parent wants their student to be the quarterback or head cheerleader. However, a team cannot function with only quarterbacks, and a band cannot function with only saxophones and percussion. The specialized instruments required a long-term commitment, and if the student was trying band for only one year, we encouraged them to choose another instrument.

At the conclusion of the event, Floyd took every student's picture and displayed posters in the hallways of the elementary school of all of the students joining the band the following year.

Beginning Band Curriculum

Floyd typically had 90–120 beginners each year, and at Hill Country, students were divided into homogeneous classes. The week before school began, the local music store delivered the instruments to the school. Floyd put name tags on instruments and method books, took new instruments out of plastic bags, removed extra cork pads, loaded reed guards, and placed the accessories in an accessory compartment. Floyd assigned each student an instrument cubby and placed their instrument in their assigned spot.

On the first day of school, Floyd took attendance and compared the class roster with her list from the instrument-interview day. Students printed their contact information on the front of an index card. Then, Floyd distributed the instruments. "We sat on the floor to assemble the instruments for the first six weeks," she said. "Instruments have less distance to fall this way!" One by one, Floyd opened each case and recorded the serial number on the index card. Students chose a colored bandana to tie on their instrument case handles. This helped distinguish their instrument from the others. "Instruments came from the same dealer and were usually the same brand, and at the end of the school day, students tended to grab the wrong instrument," she said. "The bandanas helped to identify their instrument, and students also could use the bandana to polish their flute or wipe their hands if they were using cork grease."

Floyd based the curriculum for beginning band on the Suzuki method. For the first four to six weeks, students did not use printed music, and everything was taught by watching, listening, and emulating. "I wanted to see what was happening and what the students were doing," said Floyd. "As babies, we learn to talk before we learn to read, and as a Suzuki parent, I saw how rapidly a student could progress when they learned to play by ear and we added the printed music later." Students learned how to hold the instrument, form a correct embouchure, and create a characteristic tone quality. They learned the first three notes by rote, and once they knew six simple songs, they were allowed to take their instruments home for the first time. Floyd said:

> I wanted the student to be set up correctly so they did not develop bad habits at home and the parents and siblings could recognize the songs their child was playing. We gave them a detailed handout with a series of yes and no questions: Is the metronome set at 92 BPM? Are you patting your foot when you play? Can you play the head joint, reed, and or mouthpiece for eight, ten, and twelve counts? Can you play four quarter notes in one breath? Can you play your five-note scale? Can you play "Hot Cross Buns" and "Merrily We Roll Along"? The parents listened to the student practice, circled yes or no for each question, signed the practice sheet, and the student returned the form the next day.

Floyd introduced the method book during the second six weeks, and at the end of October, she distributed the first piece for the full ensemble. Every year, the beginning band performed the same pieces. "It was a measuring stick for the students and teachers," Floyd said. "We also had many students with older siblings in the band, so they were excited to play the same music." For the holiday concert, the beginning band typically played "Jing a Ling Bells" by Sandy Feldstein and John O'Reilly, "The Hanukkah Song" by Michael Sweeney, "March of the Kings" by John Kinyon, and "Chant for Percussion" by Andrew Balent. Each section was featured and played a holiday tune or simple melody arranged as a duet. Finally, Floyd had a sight-reading demonstration for the parents. "We went through the learning process, volunteers from each section played the melody, and we finished by having the entire band play," Floyd said. "It was the parents' and administrators' favorite part of the concert because the students were becoming musically literate right before their eyes."

In April, beginners participated in a solo and ensemble concert with the other middle school in the district. Floyd chose one easy and one difficult solo for each instrument class. Beginners also played duets in small ensembles and were coached by advanced seventh and eighth graders. "The ensemble experience allowed us to teach beginners how to start with the breath and not by counting out loud, how to properly introduce the ensemble, and thank the audience when they finished their performance."

Beginners had a playing assessment two times per week. On Tuesday, they performed a line out of the method book or an excerpt of the music and, on Thursday, performed a more fundamental, technical exercise. Students recorded and then e-mailed those assessments using school-owned iPads along with a self-assessment that stated three successes and three areas of improvement. There was a detailed rubric for each playing exam, and Floyd often recorded comments or sent an e-mail confirming or amending the student's self-assessment. Since Floyd included the parents on the e-mail, she gave the student praise for accomplishments in class or discussed any ongoing problems. "Recordings tricked students into practicing because they did not want to turn in a substandard recording," she said. "It was an opportunity to submit their very best product and for me to hear every student individually."

Repertoire Selection
Floyd did not choose music for the purpose of teaching concepts such as rhythms or technique. Rather, she selected repertoire that had originality and substance. Floyd believes there is standard literature that middle school students should perform so they can continue to grow as musicians in high school. However, she still searches for new repertoire in which the composer creates new colors and unique timbres with the limited resources and the ability level of middle school students.

In 1990, the second band at Murchison Middle School premiered Frank Ticheli's "Portrait of a Clown," and the top ensemble performed Ticheli's "Fortress"—a piece dedicated to Cheryl Floyd's brother-in-law and Frank Ticheli's band director, Robert Floyd. The students worked with Ticheli, and Floyd saw the joy and excitement it brought to the rehearsal process. To honor her first class of beginners at Murchison, Floyd commissioned Ticheli to compose "Cajun Folk Songs." This project was the first in a series of commissions that included "Courtly Airs and Dances" by Ron Nelson, "Hill Country Flourishes" by Steve Barton, "Shenandoah" by Frank Ticheli, "Diamond Tide" by Viet Cuong, "Twilight in the Wilderness" by Christopher Tucker, "Undertow" by John Mackey, and several others. Floyd said:

> I attempted to find new composers who have not written for a middle school band. We asked the composer to write in their own style, but typically provided the desired length, the ranges for the brass and woodwind instruments, and instruments to highlight or avoid. We tried to have the composer present for a few rehearsals and the concert. We also incorporated students into the process; on one occasion, we sent the composer a video of the students asking questions about the piece and the compositional process. It was exciting for the parents and the community, and a great educational and musical experience for the students.

Score Study and Rehearsal Preparation

"Score study is an ongoing assessment of what the students can do versus what they must be able to do by the time of the performance," Floyd said. Her score study process not only involved a formal analysis but troubleshooting challenges. She listened to many different recordings of the piece and practiced conducting transitions, time signature changes, or other difficult passages. Floyd highlighted important aspects of the score and often showed the students her markings to teach them how to mark their music correctly. She carefully examined each line of the score, noting accidentals and considering alternative fingerings, and devised various rehearsal strategies to teach difficult concepts.

For every rehearsal, Floyd created a detailed plan for both herself and her staff. She distributed music before class and enlisted the help of other students to set up the rehearsal room. Floyd posted the order of fundamentals and pieces on the board and used a timer to pace the rehearsal and keep herself on task. When the ensemble was preparing for region contest in the second semester, Floyd sight-read and rehearsed the required march on Tuesdays and Thursdays. She devoted Mondays, Wednesdays, and Fridays to the two other pieces. "We always started by rehearsing a new section of the music and closing with a section of a piece we had already learned but needed to review and polish."

Tone

"For students to understand the fundamentals of good tone production, students need to hear what a great tone quality sounds like," Floyd asserted.

In beginning band, students listened to recordings of professional musicians, and Floyd modeled on every woodwind instrument until there was a student that could play the instrument better than her. "I was always grooming a leader or leaders in each class who could serve as models and assist if I was working with other students," she added.

Beginning band classes started with breathing exercises. Students would stand and extend their right arm as far as it could reach. Using a metronome, students inhaled for a certain amount of counts while moving the arm to the mouth. They exhaled for a certain amount of counts while sizzling and slowly extending the arm back to its starting position. "Moving the arm helped students visualize the air coming in and the air coming out," Floyd said. "It also acted as a calming device because students were coming from all different classes and activities."

Call-and-response exercises on the head joint or mouthpiece followed breathing exercises. Using a metronome, Floyd played a whole note, and the students responded. During this time, Floyd closely monitored and made adjustments to each student's embouchure. Next, Floyd articulated four quarter notes plus a whole note, and the students responded. Students would also hold one hand vertically in front of their mouth to practice articulation. If a student was having difficulty, Floyd would form a correct embouchure and articulate the rhythm on the student's hand while the student did the same on her hand. As the first month progressed, Floyd introduced dotted quarter notes and eighth-note patterns. "We laid the framework for rhythm in teaching the students the sound and feel of rhythms before reading them," she said.

In each of the call-and-response exercises, a metronome was continuously playing, and Floyd made comments between players in four counts or less. "We called this 'metronome speak'," she said. "This type of feedback kept their engagement, reinforced what they were doing well, and gave the students quick and efficient adjustments."

Once the embouchure was correct and consistent, students learned three notes by rote: flutes and oboes learned A–G–F, clarinets learned E–D–C, saxophones learned B–A–G, bassoons learned E–D–C, trumpets learned E–D–C, horns learned E–D–C, and trombones and baritones learned D–C–B-flat. Students then learned simple songs by rote that utilized those three notes. These included "Hot Cross Buns," "Merrily We Roll Along," "Mary Had a Little Lamb," and "Lightly Row." To teach any chromatic half-step, Floyd used the theme from *Jaws*, which the students called "Shark Song," and to work on harmonics, Floyd taught the bass line to "Louie, Louie." Floyd explained:

> The advantage of this method is that that we can play the song in a convenient key signature and any register of the instrument. There is no need for unison because the melodies work if they are played in thirds, fourths, or, fifths. If we want students to continue to love to play their instruments, practice faithfully, and grow from the experience, then we have to feed them a richly nourished diet with tuneful expectations.

Beginning band students continued to expand their range during the second six weeks and learned to play "America the Beautiful," "Oats, Peas, and Beans," and "Happy Birthday" from memory. Floyd gradually introduced Remington long-tone exercises and the Cichowicz Flow Studies, which were used daily in seventh and eighth grade. These exercises not only built the student's range but taught them how to smoothly navigate intervallic leaps and shift between ranges. "We wanted to make sure that every eighth-grade student had developed their range so they could be successful in high school and play more advanced literature," she said.

Intonation

According to Floyd, "Students have to play in tone before they can play in tune." In beginning band, students learned to hum to develop their aural awareness. Floyd would play a melody or fundamental exercise, and the students would hum and finger along. Brass players would hum the note before they buzzed or played. After students were set up correctly and playing with a characteristic tone, she taught the tuning tendencies of each instrument. Floyd intentionally made her instrument sharp or flat and had students match her pitch. She would then define the terms "sharp" and "flat," and allow students to experiment for themselves. Trombone, oboe, and bassoon players also used clip-on tuners to improve their intonation accuracy.

Rhythm

In the first week, Floyd taught students to pat their foot with the metronome. She had students take their shoes off so they could feel the floor underneath their foot. Then she would clap four quarter notes and students would respond by clapping four quarter notes and patting their foot. Floyd would call on students to create a rhythmic pattern and continued watching to see who maintained a steady pulse. Students also marched around the room or threw a ball with the metronome. "I learned from the Suzuki method that rhythm is in our big muscles," Floyd said. "The more we can get students moving and using muscles like their arms and legs, the quicker they can develop a sense of rhythm and pulse."

Floyd used the "count, tap, clap" system when teaching or reviewing any rhythmic pattern. Students tapped their foot to the metronome while clapping the pattern and counting using the "1-e-and-uh" system. "Our entire cluster used the same system, but I have used the Eastman system as well," Floyd said. "It does not matter which system is used, as long as it is used consistently from the beginning."

Technique

To learn the treble and bass clefs, students recited a "lines and spaces" chant with a metronome that included hand and body motions:

> *E–G–B–D–F, E–G–B–D–F,*
> *These are the lines of the treble clef.*
> *F–A–C–E, face to you and me,*
> *These are the spaces of the treble clef.*
> *G–B–D–F–A, G–B–D–F–A,*
> *These are the lines of the bass clef.*
> *All cows eat grass, all cars eat gas,*
> *These are the spaces of the bass clef.*

Likewise, students played "master of the alphabet," an activity in which students began on any note of the musical alphabet and said the note names in ascending and descending order with a metronome. Once students began reading out of the method book, they would say the note names in rhythm with a metronome, while moving their fingers accordingly. Floyd stood behind the class to see if the students were reading the music and performing the task correctly. "I had many reluctant readers from elementary school," she said, "but I learned that if students could say the note names in rhythm, with a metronome, while putting down the correct fingers, they could eventually read music."

46

Floyd taught students to hold the instrument with the correct hand position in the first week of beginning band. She told flute players to have "ballerina fingers and a ballerina's arms" as a reminder of how to hold the instrument. Once students assembled their instrument while seated on the floor, they practiced silent finger drills to set up the correct hand position. Similarly, beginning clarinets would practice "doodlettes," an exercise developed by clarinet pedagogue Ray Chapa to reinforce correct hand position and develop technical dexterity. Students played, in quarter notes, B-flat–C–C-sharp–C below the staff, and repeated the pattern several times. They added the register keys to play F–G–G-sharp–G in the second octave. Then, students lifted the first finger to play D–E–F–E in the third octave. "This exercise introduced the third octave early on," Floyd said. "It was not pretty, but students were not afraid of the third octave when we learned register slurs and scales in the second semester."

After the first six weeks of beginning band, all students could play two five-note scales and saxophones could play their concert B-flat scale and their concert B-flat scale in thirds. The second six weeks were devoted to building range and learning one-octave scales. "We always played the first scale in quarter notes, and students could earn extra credit if they played the scale in eighth notes," she said. "Bonus points are free for the teacher, and they help the student's grade and encourages them to learn to practice and challenge themselves." Starting in seventh grade, as flutes were learning to play their G-major scale, Floyd used a technique she learned from flute pedagogue Patricia George, called "running the G." They were taught the wrong fingerings for D–E–F-sharp–G on purpose, which forced them to create the correct aperture that allowed the notes to speak clearly.

By the end of sixth grade, the majority of students could play their concert B-flat, E-flat, A-flat, and F scales with appropriate octaves and would earn extra credit for additional octaves. In seventh and eighth grade, students practiced scales in a series that included the full range scale, playing the scale in thirds, and playing the scale in the Clarke Studies pattern. Floyd would review one key signature a week, but did not teach all twelve major scales. She said:

> In the first semester, we reviewed the required scales for the region band audition. We then added key signatures chromatically, but I only taught the scales that applied to the music or the etudes we were practicing in class.

I learned, over time, that if I wanted my students to have great technique, they had to practice; if I wanted them to practice, I always had to give them something to practice, whether it was a scale series, an etude, or an excerpt of music.

Words of Wisdom

Floyd encourages middle school band directors to hold students to a high expectation, challenge them on a daily basis, and give them as much information as possible in middle school. She said:

I once heard a speaker say that we should never dumb down the music to the age group that learns best. Our job is to set students up to be successful musicians, and that means our job does not end in eighth grade. I continue playing my instrument and always try to see the bigger picture because it allows me to focus on what I love doing: teaching students and making music.

Eileen Fraedrich

"Teach joyfully, and teach with purpose."

Eileen Fraedrich is currently in her thirty-third year of teaching band in Fairfax County, Virginia. She earned her bachelor's degree in music education from Ithaca College and received her master of arts degree from George Mason University.

Program Structure

Fairfax County Public Schools are divided into five regions, and each region resembles a pyramid that consists of one high school, one or two middle schools, and six to ten elementary schools. Band begins in fifth grade at the elementary school, and elementary band directors are itinerant; they are assigned to two, three, or four elementary schools by a county administrator. Each elementary school band director has one "base school," which is usually his or her largest school or the one where the teacher spends the most time.

After graduating from Ithaca College, Eileen Fraedrich was hired as an assistant band director at a secondary school in Fairfax County, where she taught middle and high school band as well as elementary strings. She became a full-time elementary school teacher shortly after, and her current base school is at Orange Hunt Elementary School. Enrollment at Orange Hunt is close to 1,000 students in kindergarten through sixth grade, and 150–180 students participate in band. Fraedrich teaches at Orange Hunt in the morning, and her afternoon assignments have varied over the years as scheduling needs have changed. Three days a week, Fraedrich is assisted by another itinerant band director.

Students at Orange Hunt have band class once a week and Fraedrich teaches one fifth-grade and one sixth-grade class each day. The school is on a block schedule in which each grade level attends "specials" (band/strings, general music, art, physical education, and foreign language) during the same one-hour block each day. Each specials class meets once a week and Fraedrich organizes students into specials groups based on their instrument choice. There are twenty to thirty students in each specials group, and some classes are homogeneous, while others have mixed instrumentation. These students, combined with the orchestra students, then attend the rest of their specials classes together throughout the week.

With proximity to Washington D.C., all branches of the military are represented in the Orange Hunt community. On Veterans Day, the band performs at three assemblies honoring veterans and active military members. They always play "The Star-Spangled Banner" along with several other selections. "It is always a challenge to prepare this music in time for a November concert, but it is worth it," Fraedrich said. "The entire community attends, and it gives us something exciting to work towards from the first day of the school year."

For the winter concert, Fraedrich began a tradition fifteen years ago where the beginners perform a skit based on the children's folk song character Aunt Rhodie. She explained:

> By December, the beginners have learned about six notes and are ready to perform. Each year, I write a play based on Aunt Rhodie, the main character in the children's folk song. The play features a cast of teachers, including our principal and assistant principal, and weaves about ten of the beginning band tunes from the method book into a storyline. We have done "Aunt Rhodie in Jurassic Park," "Aunt Rhodie Goes to Disneyworld," "Happy Birthday Aunt Rhodie," and "Aunt Rhodie Goes to Hogwarts." The "actors" make it into something special, with much laughter and hilarity. The beginners play the melody on all of the pieces, and I arrange a harmonic accompaniment for the advanced students. With props and costumes, it is a fun show and easy to prepare. At the end of the concert, the beginners play "Jingle Bells" with the advanced band.

A spring concert occurs in June, near the end of the school year. The beginners and advanced students combine to play six pieces, and the advanced students play three pieces by themselves. Each year, the sixth graders perform a piece dedicated to their class, and Fraedrich honors them with a slide show, featuring a photo of each student holding his or her instrument.

Many of the students participate in an annual solo and ensemble festival. Interested students typically play from the *Standard of Excellence Festival Solos* book. "This book provides a variety of solos for beginning and intermediate players, which get progressively more challenging," Fraedrich said. "The accompanying CD allows the student to hear a professional playing the piece and also provides the piano accompaniment to use for practice or performance." For duets and trios, Fraedrich uses the first and second books of *Alfred's Basic Solos and Ensembles* and *Standard of Excellence Festival Ensembles*. Fraedrich also offers a chamber-ensemble experience for interested students. She explained:

> Any fifth or sixth grader can participate, and we practice several times during recess, then perform as a group at the contest. It is an excellent way for students to experience solo and ensemble festival and appeals to many students who feel nervous performing solos. Since the large groups perform early in the morning, we have a tradition of eating breakfast together before the festival, so it is also a great bonding experience.

Additional Instruction

Orange Hunt does not offer private lessons, but interested students typically take lessons from the many service band members who teach nearby. Fraedrich also provides additional instruction during lunch, recess, or before school. "I have door duty every morning, so it is not unusual for students to stand at the door with me, playing their instruments, as other students arrive at school," she said. "It is a great advertisement for the band!"

Recruitment

"Recruitment is the first step to having a great band program," Fraedrich said. "I cannot overemphasize its importance." Throughout her career, Fraedrich has tried various approaches to recruitment—going into each classroom, having a large assembly, demonstrating the instruments herself, having her students demonstrate, having high school students demonstrate, fall recruitment, spring recruitment, and more. However, she has learned that recruitment begins much earlier. She said:

> Recruitment begins when the students are still too young to begin band—when they hear the band perform at concerts and school events, or when they see me in the hall or on door duty with an instrument in hand or working with band students. We are promoting band when the students see their peers playing instruments as they walk past the band room or see their friends on the "Band Wall of Fame" in the hallway. They hear the band when I take a class into the cafeteria to play a song during lunch or when their classmate wins the opportunity to guest-conduct the band as part of the PTA Silent Auction. Especially in an elementary school, recruitment is an ongoing process, and visibility is crucial.

At Orange Hunt, the recruitment process is in three phases: the assembly, the follow-up, and the parent meeting. There is one assembly for each grade level, and about thirty of Fraedrich's students will dress up in the high school band uniforms and march into the assembly. As prospective students arrive, Fraedrich plays Sousa marches, and the students walk through a hallway of music stands decorated with music posters she has collected over the years. At the beginning of the program, Fraedrich tells prospective students to remember three things as they listen to the performers:

> I tell them they do not need to know anything about music—no note-reading, not how to make a sound, not even the name of the instrument—I am going to teach them that. I have found that some students come in worried about past problems they have had in general music class. The second reminder is that band takes place during school; they do not need to stay after school. The students in this area are very busy, having many activities after school. Knowing that it is not an after-school commitment is important to them. The last reminder is that band is free. We provide the books, music, and instruction as part of the district program. Students rent an instrument from local music stores for very reasonable prices. If they cannot afford to rent an instrument and are eligible for the free-and-reduced lunch program, the Fairfax school system will provide one.

Fraedrich has her students demonstrate each of the instruments, playing fun and recognizable songs. For the flute, Fraedrich brings in a soda bottle or water bottle and shows them how to get a sound by blowing across the top. "I ask them to go home and try it, and then tell me if they were able to do it," she added. For the clarinet, Fraedrich shows them how the fingerings for "Hot Crossed Buns" and "Mary Had a Little Lamb" are the same as their recorder fingerings, emphasizing that they will be able to go home the first day and play these songs. For French horn, Fraedrich shows them how it is one long tube coiled up and pretends to uncoil it, stretching the tube across the room. For all brass instruments, Fraedrich shows students how to create a buzz. "I have them lick their lips, say the letter M silently, blow through, and press their lips together to get a buzz," she said. For trombone, Fraedrich highlights the uniqueness of the slide, with students demonstrating glissandi. She always calls one volunteer from the audience to try buzzing, play a glissando, and guess where various positions would be on the instrument. Fraedrich then answers questions and passes out the registration letter for the students to take home. Overall, she believes spending time on each instrument, sharing fun facts about the band, and choosing recognizable demonstration pieces has a profound effect on the band instrumentation.

On the days following the recruitment assembly, Fraedrich visits each class separately and allows students to try out each instrument. She meets with them individually, briefly screening for instrument choices and answering their questions. Students are allowed to play their first choice of instruments, and she does not put a cap or limit on the instrumentation. Fraedrich then sends a letter home with information on acquiring the student's instrument choice. She attaches flyers from the local music stores with information on rental, as well as a list of required equipment.

Before the start of band class, there is a parent meeting in which Fraedrich demonstrates the instruments once again, discusses specific information about the band program, and answers questions. "My goal is for the parents to leave feeling as excited about their child's participation in the band as the children are themselves," she said.

In previous years, the recruitment program started at the beginning of the school year. However, last year, Fraedrich began in the spring, after the final concert of the year. She said:

> We just had our concert, so it was fresh in the minds of the students, and
> I was able to use the concert as another opportunity to show them the

instruments, to generate interest and excitement, and to invite them to play in the band. There are pros and cons to spring recruitment versus fall, but overall it did make the beginning of the school year much smoother, and we can start our band classes on the first day of school.

Retention

Fraedrich works closely with the directors in her pyramid to make the transition easier from elementary to middle to high school. Each year, there is a joint concert hosted by the high school and middle school bands. All sixth graders from the six elementary schools in the pyramid are invited to participate, and the booster organizations provide a pizza dinner. They perform two pieces with the top high school and middle school band students. The middle school and high school bands also perform pieces on their own, which showcases the musical progression from elementary to middle school to high school.

Fraedrich's students can also participate in an area honor band. This ensemble is an extracurricular band that meets weekly over several months, for students in the six elementary schools within the pyramid. They rehearse at the middle school, and the middle school director leads the group, which allows the students to become familiar with them and the middle school building. The honor band also allows students to meet and make friends with students from other schools.

Lastly, each year in early spring, Fraedrich has a "band picnic" in which students have lunch with the middle school band director in the Orange Hunt band room. The director shows a slideshow, talks with students about what they can expect in middle school band, and will often bring cookies or small gifts for the students, such as wristbands with the name of the middle school.

Rehearsal Preparation

Fraedrich strongly believes that planning and preparation for a rehearsal will determine the success of the rehearsal. Each day, the room is set up before the students enter, and name tags are placed on the music stands. The name tags are color-coded by weekday for easier distribution, and Fraedrich uses them as a classroom management tool, pairing weaker players with stronger players or moving disruptive students. She places a pencil on each music stand along with a practice record and any additional music. This consistent routine not only minimizes distractions during rehearsal but sets the expectation for behavior and proper rehearsal etiquette.

Before a concert, Fraedrich will schedule several full band rehearsals. "These are very exciting for the students, as it will be the first time they get to hear all of the sections of the band playing together," she said. "With over 180 students combining, there is the possibility of chaos unless I have prepared." Fraedrich creates a detailed routine for the rehearsal to run smoothly. She must first get approval for the rehearsal dates with the classroom teachers since students will leave class for rehearsal. Fraedrich must also reserve the cafeteria or gym well in advance since they are the only spaces large enough for the full ensemble. Fraedrich begins preparing students by reviewing and practicing behavior expectations in class. She will often have the students play through music with a sample recording so that they can hear how their part will fit in with the other sections. A few days before the rehearsal, Fraedrich makes a seating chart. She is mindful of balance and sound, as well as to which students will do well sitting together. Fraedrich makes name tags for the rehearsal, color-coded by instrument, and organizes them for quick distribution.

On the day before the rehearsal, Fraedrich posts signs on every classroom door reminding the students to bring their instruments the next day. She will often have the classroom teachers pass out reminder notes for the students to put in their planners. An e-mail is also sent to remind parents. "Having a band e-mail list is a must," said Fraedrich. "It takes time at the beginning of the year to compile this distribution list, but the benefit to the band program is well worth the effort involved." On the day of the rehearsal, Fraedrich informs the custodian she will set up after lunch, as this may impact their cleaning routine. When the students arrive, the room is ready with chairs, stands, nametags, and a rehearsal order posted on the wall. Playing time is maximized by focusing on balance and fitting all parts together accurately. If the rehearsal is going well, Fraedrich might invite an administrator or teacher to watch so that the students can practice performing for an audience. "By the time of the actual rehearsal, everything is in place for a successful practice," she said. "The hard work comes beforehand!"

Repertoire Selection

Fairfax County provides funds for the purchase of music and method books, with a set amount per student in the program. When selecting method books, Fraedrich considers the music selections, the overall design, the order in which the material is presented, starting pitches for the various instruments, how the book handles the unique needs of the French horn and oboe, and additional resources available. She currently uses the first and second books in the *Essential Elements* series. She said:

> I like the way the book presents new information, the order of the starting pitches (concert F, E-flat, D, C, B-flat), the alternate pages provided for beginning oboe and French horn, and the uncluttered design. *Essential Elements* also provides accompaniment tracks that are available to students as a download or on CD and includes a listening library, music from many countries and composers, and supplemental trios and duets.

Over the years, Fraedrich has used most of the available method books and often supplements them with personal materials. She has created exercises for crossing the break on clarinet, note-reading drills, composition, and any other skill students need in order to improve.

Tone

Fraedrich believes students need first to be aware of what a characteristic tone quality sounds like before they can produce it themselves. She frequently demonstrates and models on the instrument she is teaching and has students listen to professional musicians and ensembles. "Students need to be able to describe what they hear, so we use adjectives like *full*, *solid*, *mature*, *warm*, *round*, *harsh*, and *splatty*," she said. "Being aware of the sound they are producing and being able to compare it to the model with descriptive language through guided questions is an ongoing process."

Once students have learned the first five notes, students perform a daily exercise in which they play a whole note followed by a half note, quarter note, and an eighth note. As they are playing, Fraedrich encourages students to use enough air to fill up the instrument and produce a full, rich sound. "In every exercise, we have to draw attention to the quality of sound students are making and constantly remind them about posture, embouchure, keeping the throat open in an 'ah' shape, and taking full, deep breaths."

In the second semester, students learn their chromatic scale, and, for motivation, students can pass-off specific exercises in the method book to earn a spot on the "Wall of Fame." They can also continue to pass-off exercises to join the "Wall of Amazing Fame" and the "Wall of Unbelievably Amazing Fame." Fraedrich added:

> I use construction paper to cut out ribbons and color-code them by the instrument. It is a badge of honor for the students to see their name on the bulletin board and motivation for other students to continue practicing. My band room is in a central hallway in the school, so it also serves as a recruitment tool because the younger students see our accomplishments.

Intonation

Just as with tone quality, Fraedrich believes students need first to be aware and be able to describe the meaning of intonation. "After we develop a consistent and characteristic tone, I explain the purpose of a tuner, how it works, and the definition of sharp and flat based on the location of the needle," she said. "Then, I will have a student play one note, and we will adjust their instrument in both directions, so other students see and hear the difference." As students continue learning more notes in the first and second year, they learn when and how they need to adjust the instrument or their embouchure to fix the intonation.

Rhythm

Fraedrich utilizes several games to teach rhythm. For example, at the end of class, she will often play "rhythm bingo." She creates eight different bingo cards with assorted rhythms in each square, and students are given one card along with a sheet that has all the rhythms from the eight cards. Fraedrich plays a rhythm on the snare drum, and the first person to get bingo wins a prize. She will also split the class into two teams and play "rhythm baseball." One person from each team goes to the board, Fraedrich plays a rhythm, and the first person to correctly dictate the rhythm gets to move one base for their team. She will perform more complex rhythms for doubles, triples, or home runs. Fraedrich also has various note values or rhythms printed on index cards and a student will arrange the cards in a random order. Everybody in the class will count, clap, or sizzle the rhythm while tapping their foot. Another game she plays is called "snake," in which each student plays one measure of an exercise or rhythm sheet, and the class has to seamlessly play the exercise without any breaks. "It seems small, but it is a big celebration if the entire class is able to do it," she said. To that, she added:

> Anything can be made into a game, and these are great ways to change up the routine and turn something boring into something fun and exciting. Teachers have to be able to improvise—to see the problem preventing the student from reaching the goal and find a creative, fun way to reach it. Teachers also have to understand what students think is fun. They love to get prizes, even as silly as a scratch-and-sniff sticker, and they love to work together to try to achieve a goal. It fulfills an *esprit de corps* and makes them want to come back to class the next week.

Technique

Fraedrich plays similar games with her students to develop technical coordination and dexterity. However, she first establishes correct hand position and how to hold the instrument with no physical limitation. With any technical exercise or piece of music, she often divides the music into smaller sections, as students can be overwhelmed at first. She said:

> A piece like "The Star-Spangled Banner," for example, can be very intimidating to a beginning band student. Therefore, I will divide the music into sections based on the verses. We will learn and practice each section very slowly and accurately, and gradually put them together. I then point out that the second verse is just a repeat of the first. It is essential for young students to make this connection and learn that hard tasks are easy if they are broken down into simple, manageable parts.

Words of Wisdom

Fraedrich believes that being a lifelong learner is essential in the teaching profession and in life. She encourages directors to take advantage of opportunities for learning and interacting with other band teachers, such as state and national music conventions or teacher training events. "I feel fortunate to have access to great classes, in-services, workshops, online training, and conferences, many of which are offered through my school system and are free to teachers," she said. "After these events, I always feel revitalized with new ideas and experiences to try in my classroom."

She has recently attended workshops on Google Classroom and found new ways to extend teaching beyond the walls of the band class, thanks to teaching partners who are younger and more current on new technologies. She also recently took a guitar course for teachers, offered through NAfME, which taught her about playing and teaching the guitar and gave her new ideas about teaching in general. As a result, she began a free community guitar program at a local church.

If these kinds of learning opportunities are not readily available, Fraedrich encourages directors to consider hosting an event for other directors in the area. She said:

> We have a band directors' association in Fairfax County that plans some outstanding teacher training events. One was called "Trick or Treat" because it took place around Halloween, and each director came with a "teaching trick" to share and a favorite piece of band music, which we sight-read. Having the opportunity to interact with other band directors is invaluable. We can never stop learning!

Each day, Fraedrich strives to teach joyfully, teach with purpose, and provide a fun, positive experience for her students in which they are excited about their progress. She said:

> When the novelty of playing a new instrument wears off, we have to continue to maintain the student's motivation and do something completely different and out of the ordinary. One day each year I will set up the chairs like an airplane, give the students boarding passes as they enter the classroom, and use songs in the method book to travel and learn about different countries. Students can even win fake refreshments if they correctly answer questions, and we experience turbulence if they do not play well. On another day, I set up the room to look like a time machine, and we travel to different musical time periods. We play a song by a composer from the Renaissance or Classical period and connect music history with world history. It sounds silly, but I have learned over the years that young students still like to play pretend. Therefore, I give much thought and energy to planning fun, creative, excellent lessons. It is my hope and intention that every day, my students will be thinking, "I cannot wait to get to band class!"

Chris Gleason

"I don't teach music; I teach through music."

Chris Gleason earned his bachelor's degree in music education from the University of Wisconsin-Eau Claire and his master's degree from the University of Wisconsin-LaCrosse. He has been the director of bands at Patrick Marsh Middle School in Sun Prairie, Wisconsin since 2004.

Program Structure

As the son of a band director, Chris Gleason spent his childhood in his father's band room in Arcadia, Wisconsin. He began teaching in a small school in East Troy, Wisconsin and, two years later, moved back home to take over for his father upon his retirement. Gleason spent five years in LaCrosse, Wisconsin before moving to Sun Prairie to teach at Patrick Marsh Middle School. Located outside of Madison, Sun Prairie is the fastest growing school district in Wisconsin. Patrick Marsh Middle School was initially built for grades six through eight but became a sixth and seventh-grade campus in 2010 when the district built a new high school. Approximately 600 students attend Patrick Marsh, with around 240 students enrolled in band. With such growth, Gleason experiences frequent changes within his school district. He said, "The key is to stay flexible and focused on the core philosophy of education in the face of constant change."

Gleason and his colleague teach three heterogeneous sixth-grade glasses that meet every other day for forty-five minutes. Two seventh-grade concert bands meet every day for forty-five minutes and are divided based on their schedule. A sixth-grade jazz band meets once a week after school and a seventh-grade jazz band meets twice a week before school. Gleason also teaches a seventh-grade jazz combo once a week after school. Students can enroll in band and either orchestra or choir, and since electives meet during the same period, students might go to band one day and orchestra or choir the next. Gleason said:

> The philosophy of the program is to allow students the option to be in more than one music class. However, families are asked to carefully consider this option, as all of the music programs are rigorous. We have found that some students excel in this setting and others find that it is too much and eventually settle on one music class or ensemble.

Additional Instruction

Each week, every sixth and seventh-grade band student has a ten-minute private lesson with either Gleason or his colleague. Lessons occur before or after school, during band, or during study hall. On rare occasions, Gleason pulls students from academic classes such as social studies. Lessons are consistent from week to week, so teachers and students can anticipate the absence from class. Gleason also started a private lesson academy for students seeking more advanced instruction. He hires local professionals and students from the University of Wisconsin-Madison through the booster organization. Approximately forty students are involved in the private lesson academy.

On Friday mornings before school, students participate in instrument-specific chamber ensembles such as flute choir, clarinet choir, and trumpet ensemble. They rehearse for thirty-five minutes, and private lesson instructors or community members volunteer their time to teach these ensembles.

Gleason believes it is essential for students to have the opportunity to learn within multiple settings. "If you look at our program, each student is heard individually, performs in chamber ensembles, and then plays in the full ensemble," he said. "In this setup, no student gets lost in the mix."

Concert Schedule

The bands at Patrick Marsh perform four concerts each year. Since fundamentals are the primary focus at the beginning of the year and songs are often very short, Gleason invites faculty colleagues to record themselves playing a few notes on an instrument they have never played before. For example, Gleason will teach his math colleague how to hold and play a few notes on the flute. He shows a video of the teacher performing at the concert just before the sixth-grade flute section performs. "The expression on the student's faces is priceless," Gleason said. "The students feel more confident with their performance, knowing that they will sound better than their teachers. Also, the faculty realizes the difficulty and complexity of what our students do."

For the winter concert, Gleason features a guest soloist with the seventh-grade band. He said:

> How do I get my students to play softer and more delicately? How do I motivate them to play with a better sound and listen more carefully? I have them listen and work with a professional musician. It not only features our private lesson teachers or local professionals but teaches the students how to accompany, and it helps improve their aural skills.

The chamber ensembles that rehearse on Friday mornings before school perform a concert in the early Spring. This concert also features a special performance by the "parent band." One month before the concert, sixth-grade students are asked to teach one of their parents how to play their instrument. The parents gather for one thirty-minute rehearsal before the concert and perform a few songs from the method book. Regarding the purpose of this ensemble, Gleason said:

> Students learn best when they teach. More importantly, parents get to experience the intricacy of what their child is doing and have a deeper appreciation of our philosophy and process. The priceless moments come when I have been continuously working on posture with a student, and you see a video of him scolding his father to fix his posture.

The concert bands also participate in a district "band-o-rama" concert in the spring that features all sixteen bands from the middle and high schools. The concert includes a mass performance of "The Star-Spangled Banner" and "On Wisconsin" by the combined ensembles. This concert tries to unify the community by celebrating the district administration, highlighting the elementary school music teachers, or featuring a guest conductor or composer.

Since 2009, the final concert of the year has included the premiere of a new work commissioned by Patrick Marsh Middle School. Through grant writing, community donations, and organizing a noncompetitive performance festival at a local indoor waterpark, Gleason has commissioned prominent composers such as Samuel Hazo, John Mackey, Brian Balmages, Michael Sweeney, Alex Shapiro, and Andrew Boysen. Although Gleason contracts the composer years in advance, he involves seventh graders in the creative and compositional process. Gleason video-records students offering their ideas and inspirations for the piece at the beginning of the year. Each student shares their idea and says why it is a good idea and what compositional techniques they would use if they were writing the piece. The video is played at the fall concert and also is sent to the composer so they can meet and learn about the students. The students and composer continue to interact throughout the year as the composer completes initial drafts.

The first piece Gleason commissioned was Samuel Hazo's "Blue and Green Music," which he based on the paintings of Sun Prairie native Georgia O'Keeffe. The students learned about the history of the O'Keeffe family and took a trip to the art museum to study O'Keeffe's paintings, and Gleason invited O'Keeffe's family to the premiere. Composer Alex Shapiro asked students to explore and record various sounds they could make with rocks, which ultimately became the underlying track to accompany the piece. These experiences have been definitive moments in Gleason's career. He said:

> Once you commission a composition, a bond is created between the composer, the students, and the piece of music. By studying the origin of creativity and being involved in the process, my students have been able to understand not just the technical elements but also the context. Understanding the meaning behind the music has led to an entirely new affect in their performance.

Recruitment

Gleason recruits students from four and a half elementary schools. In the first semester, the seventh-grade band visits each elementary school and gives a forty-minute presentation and performance to the fifth-grade class. Gleason has students demonstrate the instruments, performs Andrew Balent's "Introducing the Band," and even allows a few fifth-grade students to conduct. Gleason directs students to the school district website, which has a page called "Join the Band!" This webpage includes a video that introduces the instruments and a twenty-page booklet that outlines specifics of the band program and answers frequently asked questions. "We modeled this after corporate branding and tried to create a place that shows families that they are entering into a family and a community that is not just for one year," Gleason said.

Gleason and his colleagues visit all nine district elementary schools during the second semester for mouthpiece "sampling." "We used to call it mouthpiece testing, but with the connotations of that word in our current society, sampling was a better choice," Gleason said. Every fifth grader samples mouthpieces and a director provides an overall rating. "A fifth grader has never had the opportunity to buzz their lips to play an instrument properly," he said. "But once they experience that sensation and work one-on-one with a director, they are more likely to sign up."

In May, fifth-grade parents use Google Forms to sign up for an "instrument fitting" on two different evenings after school. Students try out several instruments that initially catch their eye. "We want them to gravitate towards their interests and hope they will be successful," Gleason said. "However, this is not the last stop, and we are savvy enough to know what to look for in players of specific instruments." For example, if students are interested in brass, care is taken to listen for potential in each student's buzzing. He explained:

> Buzzing a trombone or euphonium mouthpiece is most natural for students. Buzzing a trumpet or tuba, however, means supporting the buzz in a way that students have not necessarily done before. Consequently, students will feel less excited about these instruments when trying them for the first time.

In sixth grade, the instrument choices are limited to flute, clarinet, trumpet, trombone, euphonium, and tuba. Individual students are then invited to play bass clarinet, French horn, and double reeds in December of the first year. At the end of sixth grade, any student can audition for alto, tenor, or baritone saxophone. Gleason also holds two percussion workshops in which fifth graders can explore mallets and snare pads. The students that can listen to directions, work with other students, and process information quickly are typically the ones selected to play percussion.

Curriculum

Gleason is a strong proponent of the Comprehensive Musicianship through Performance (CMP) project that Wisconsin initiated in 1977. According to the Wisconsin Music Education Association:

> In the CMP process, the rehearsal is seen as a laboratory where students can develop an understanding of musical concepts such as expression, melody, rhythm, harmony, texture, timbre, and form by being involved in a variety of roles including performing, improvising, arranging, composing, conducting, and analyzing music.

Gleason and his district colleagues have developed a vertically aligned curriculum that consists of a series of proficiency statements and consistent gradations from elementary to high school. These learning outcomes conform to the CMP model and satisfy administrative objectives; they are measured, time-based, performance oriented, and easily manageable by the student.

However, for Gleason, curriculum goes beyond music. He aims to teach beyond the musical objectives to include higher-order creative thinking and practical behavioral skills. For example, in beginning band, students learn how to problem solve and function like a professional. They learn classroom procedures, rehearsal focus, literacy, and how to build strong practice habits. He said:

> I use Daniel Coyle's book, *The Talent Code*, to teach students about myelin—the fatty substance or sheath that wraps around a child's neural networks. We learn how to break down complicated tasks into smaller intervals and build myelin through multiple repetitions. By teaching the students what skill is and *how* to practice, they have the tools to be more effective. The students also better understand *why* they need to practice. Knowing the reason is vital because students need to decide to practice on their own. Motivation lasts the longest and is more meaningful when it is intrinsic.

Gleason has a poster in his band room titled "Questions About Questions." The purpose is to teach sixth graders to ask themselves a series of questions before asking a director: Is it an emergency? Is this the right time? Is this on topic? Is this good for the group? Will you find out anyway? Gleason referenced Alfie Kohn, who said, "Talk less, ask more." To that, he added, "The art of asking questions is hugely important. The best teachers have teeth marks on their tongue because they are constructing knowledge through questions. If we as teachers ask questions that promote higher-level thinking, the students will imitate that back."

Gleason makes it a priority to teach his students empathy, community, and compassion through band. "Every seventh grader needs to put themselves in other people's shoes and understand how they can contribute positively to society," he said. "I teach those qualities through music." For instance, when Gleason performed a transcription of Pavel Chesnokov's "Salvation is Created," the students studied and discussed the historical context of the work.

> Chesnokov never heard his work performed because the Russian government banned sacred music. When they destroyed the church he worked at, Chesnokov stopped writing music altogether. I asked my students to put themselves in the composer's shoes, to relate it to their own lives, and recognize how that informs the meaning of the text and inspiration for the piece. Through that discussion, they learned about empathy.

Similarly, Gleason used Brian Balmages' "Moscow 1941" to explore how certain groups contribute to or harm society. Students created a mission statement and an action plan to make the school community a better place. They started the "Sit Down Club," in which they sat with a different group of students each day at lunch. They even made t-shirts, and when Gleason's principal asked him what they were doing, he responded, "They are doing band." Gleason elaborated:

> It's not just about the notes; it's about going beyond notes. They are going to play well, but at the end of the day, I want them to learn something about themselves or the world we live in and how they can be a better person.

Assessment
As a whole, Gleason does not participate in any competitive events with his students. He said:

> I love Daniel Pink's book *Drive,* as it has helped shape my understanding of how and why people are motivated. After students perform, the first thing they want to know is a rating. However, I think the focus needs to be on the

feedback and the experience. I believe competitive events often force students and teachers to take shortcuts, and we lose the essence of why we are there in the first place. I used to do practice charts, but I realized kids were not playing better. I was just bribing them with stickers, and they were faking it. I believe the more you reward, the less interest they take in whatever they have to do to get the reward. The more you make it about the trophy or the score, the less interest they take in earning that. They want to know the least amount they have to do to get that reward or grade.

Therefore, Gleason promotes purpose, mastery, and individual engagement by allowing students to have a choice. "This creates a sense of purposefulness that is relevant to their own lives," he said. "I have found the more meaningful it is to them, the more they want to participate and go beyond the standard."

At the beginning of the year, students create both an individual and ensemble rubric to measure progress and success. "Students should never receive a rubric because the teacher owns it, not them," Gleason said. "Students need to establish the criteria for excellence. The more they own the rubric, the better the results." There are four levels of measurement on most of Gleason's rubrics: exceeds proficiency, proficient, approaching proficiency, and does not meet expectations. Gleason asks students to score themselves on various ensemble skills, including being on time to class. Most students say "exceeds," and Gleason points out that arriving on time is actually "proficient," while arriving early "exceeds." Students then make a detailed plan on how they can be more efficient before class begins.

Other ensemble skills in the rubric include instrument and supplies, wise warmups, rehearsal focus, questions, instrument, posture, and instrument care. Gleason said:

> We try to make the rubrics fun by using things like trains. Students would walk into a private lesson and admit they derailed (does not meet expectations) on a few items while they were full steam ahead on others (exceeds expectations). In this system, students create the idea of excellence and can assess it for themselves.

Using Google Forms, students also individually assess rhythmic skills, technique, and tone quality each academic quarter. Gleason adds his comments, and at the following private lesson, Gleason and the student discuss each category and make a plan for the next quarter. Using Autocrat, a Google add-on, the student's answers as well as Gleason's comments are merged, sorted, and e-mailed to each student's family. Parents receive multiple pages of narrative feedback for their child, rather than getting an arbitrary grade at the end of the semester. "I have found this is way more effective than a practice chart because students intrinsically own this kind of assessment, understand where they are in the spectrum of mastery, and have a plan for how they are going to get there," he said.

Score Study and Rehearsal Preparation
Gleason uses the CMP model as the basis for his score study and rehearsal preparation. He analyzes every element of music (form, timbre, texture, melody, harmony, rhythm, etc.), and when he finishes, he summarizes the work in one or two sentences. "The idea is to understand what element of music is driving the work and what is the result," he said.

Gleason also believes speculation about the music and asking why the composer made certain decisions is an essential aspect of score study. He attempts to answer those questions by studying the historical context and origin of the piece in detail. "You have to pull back all of the layers because it leads to a deeper level of understanding," he said. If he is unable to come up with the answer, he presents the questions to the students. "Kids need to understand ambiguity, as this stimulates their creativity and imagination while encouraging them to seek the answers themselves."

Before distributing the parts, Gleason will have students listen to a recording and map out the architecture of the work to understand its construction. Similarly, he will extract important musical elements and melodic themes, and arrange them for every instrument. For example, when introducing Andrew Boysen's "Tricycle," Gleason played the five notes that formulate the core of the work and asked students to imagine a composition that only used those notes. He did not answer, but for the next week had the students create different ways of ordering and playing those five notes. The following week, he added countermelodies and harmonies. The following week, Gleason asked students to find a piece that was composed using only those five notes. While some students were successful, Gleason then passed out the parts to "Tricycle." "The students were instantly sold before ever listening to it or playing it," he said, "because they understood and appreciated the creativity needed to construct such a piece."

Tone

Gleason relates learning to play with a proper tone quality to how we initially learn to talk. "Students have to have an aural example of what a characteristic tone is from the very beginning," he said. "Just like when we learn to speak or like how jazz musicians learn to improvise, we have to build skills through listening and imitating." The week before school begins, Gleason holds a camp for beginning band students called "Band Starts Now!" Students meet each morning for ninety minutes, and on the first day, there is a performance by a professional musician. "We want a quality sound to be the first thing they hear," Gleason said. Throughout the week and into the first semester, Gleason has his students compare and contrast recordings of various professionals. He explained:

> First, we have to imitate and then we have to extend. I developed as a musician by imitating great tuba players and mixing those qualities into something that was innately my style. I want my students to find what they love, understand why they love it, and become their own mixture.

During the mini-camp, students develop the physical aspects of playing by establishing a proper posture and working on various breathing exercises. Gleason referenced legendary tubist and brass pedagogue Arnold Jacobs' book *Wind and Song* for teaching students to imagine wind blowing through their instrument. He also incorporates exercises from the popular DVD, *The Breathing Gym*.

Students then learn how to set the embouchure correctly, although daily reinforcement is necessary. Gleason uses Coach's Eye, an app that can take video or photos, playback in slow motion, zoom in and out, and record commentary. Gleason and the student will take videos and pictures of correct and incorrect embouchures in their weekly private lessons, and students can use it as a resource while practicing at home.

Gleason does not use a comprehensive method book with his beginners. Instead, he uses the first and second books of the *Student Instrumental Course* published by Belwin. This series contains instrument-specific exercises to develop proper tone, range, and technique. He said:

We have to be mindful about whether we are teaching the best notes for that particular instrument from the beginning. We also have to be mindful about whether we are teaching songs or teaching the instrument. You can get through the method book and learn to play songs but haven't learned to play or be skillful on their instrument.

While students work through the first and second Belwin books in sixth and seventh grade, the full ensemble classes have a series of warm-up exercises that include long tones, scales, and simple songs. Gleason adapts these exercises daily to maintain student interest and engagement. For example, he will often use the "Hollywood warmups," in which a background track with sounds similar to a Hollywood soundtrack accompanies the students.

Intonation

"A student *has* to play in tone before they can be in tune," Gleason said. He has students hum and sing every day with a sustained drone, placing the speakers behind the ensemble, so students learn to listen in that direction. He uses a variety of visualizers and apps, such as Tonal Energy, Coach's Eye, or Decibel Meter to assist in ear training. He connects an iPad to his Apple TV, which allows him to walk around the classroom, sometimes taking pictures of embouchures, posture, or hand position. Gleason will also periodically use clip-on tuners but is cautious about training the eye over the ear. He said:

It is like a speedometer; it is good to have it some of the time, but you do not always need it. You want the student's ears to become their speedometer. You want them to be flexible and have the skills to adjust in different performance settings.

When Gleason does not use visualizers, students give a thumbs up or thumbs down when individuals or sections are tuning. This strategy allows Gleason to assess a student's aural awareness, and disagreements typically lead to a discussion and exploration of tuning tendencies. Gleason also frequently records students both in their private lessons and in the full ensemble rehearsal. Students provide written and verbal critique, with Gleason asking detailed questions to guide their responses. Overall, Gleason believes that students need to understand the importance of individual intonation within the context of the full ensemble. "If one person is playing the wrong note or out of tune, the entire group is wrong," he said. "We talk about this concept not to scare them but to make them aware that they are always on, all of the time.

Rhythm

To build a strong rhythmic foundation, Gleason first teaches students to have a strong inner pulse. He uses a metronome every day, but similar to a tuner, teaches students to not rely on it. "The metronome keeps everybody honest, but I want my students to be able to listen, watch, and adjust to maintain tempo," he said. Gleason will often turn down the volume while students are playing and gradually increase it to check the consistency of the pulse. During fundamentals, he encourages students to watch by dictating changes through different physical movements or facial expressions.

Gleason will analyze intricate rhythms found in the concert music and incorporate them into a warmup. For example, when he performed Andrew Boysen's "Tricycle," he wrote out the complex rhythms in 5/4 meter for the entire ensemble. He removed the time signature but added the subdivisions for sustained notes. As part of the warmup, half the students sizzled the subdivision while the other half sizzled the rhythm. He also had students create their own rhythms in 5/4 meter, adding accents and dynamics as they progressed. Gleason said:

> I want my students to have a voice in what we are doing and choice in what they get to do. I would put their composed rhythms into a program through the SMART board. Students would throw bean bags at the SMART board, and a rhythm would pop up. We would all chant, clap, and sizzle the rhythm and then find and play that rhythm in the music, so there was direct application and relevance for the student.

Technique

Gleason has found that telling a personal story is an effective and relevant way of teaching abstract concepts. He relates technical ability on an instrument to his experience learning how to hold a golf club.

> I once took golf lessons with my son, and when I tried to hold the club, the teacher looked at me and said, "No one in the world holds the club that way." If I wanted to hit the ball, I had to hold the club the proper way. Holding an instrument is the same concept; students cannot be successful

unless they have proper hand position. They hold the instrument in different ways, and students experience for themselves why one way is correct and the others are not. I then have students observe and assess each other, asking what they notice and what they would fix. The goal is to provide purpose, understanding, and relevancy for why these fundamental skills are essential.

Similarly, Gleason has a handout titled "Scales Are Fun!" that has the circle of fifths, the order of sharps and flats, and a picture of the piano keys. The purpose is for students to understand the construction of scales to produce it on their instrument. Gleason said:

> If they can understand the meaning of a key signature, the circle of fifths, and enharmonic equivalents, and then build the scale by writing and saying the note names, they can play and master any scale. Muscle memory is necessary, but physical production and recall are more attainable if they have the mental facility to understand it.

Musicianship

Gleason believes in making rehearsals purposeful and relevant to the student's life for performances to be effective and affective. For his master's thesis, he explored these qualities using the CMP model. One piece on the concert was taught using skill-based methods, and Gleason rehearsed every musical element in an objective, mechanical way. With the other piece, students not only learned the technical elements of their part, but explored the historical context of the work, analyzed the harmonic, melodic, and rhythmic elements, and completed a series of journal entries sharing their thoughts and emotions on the composition. Gleason used visualizations and analogies related to the student and the music to ignite their imaginations. At the concert, colleagues and parents said the piece that used the CMP model was more emotionally connected and had a higher aesthetic quality. "When a student feels a connection to their personal life, they not only build skills but also understand the reason the skill is necessary," he concluded. "They work harder, and this knowledge leads to more meaningful and emotional performances."

Gleason continues to use the CMP model to present subjective musical concepts in a relatable way. For example, he introduces music theory in the context of the music. He said:

Music theory cannot be bad clerical work, and the last thing students need is another worksheet. I give out the score or a page of the score, even if it is a grade -1 piece, and students will write in the note names for other instruments. If it is a lyrical piece, we will talk about why the music is beautiful. If it is the neighboring tones, we will highlight all of the neighboring tones in the piece. Or, we will talk about consonance and dissonance, and we will listen and highlight the dissonant chords. This way, it is relevant and immediately applicable.

When he was rehearsing Pavel Chesnokov's "Salvation is Created," Gleason used a large elastic band to teach students how to shape a phrase. Gleason played the choral recording of the work, and eight students moved the elastic band to the music, stretching as the music grew and contracting as the music softened. "The kinesthetic and visual experience allowed the students to see the architecture of the piece," he said. "Once they understood this, teaching them how to control their breath and sustain a good tone was easy because there was a purpose."

A few times a year, Gleason will take his students on a walk outside instead of rehearsing. He asks them to remain silent but be aware of what is around them. When they return to the classroom, he asks them what they noticed.

Some will say they saw four geese or some would hear car horns, but every student notices something different. This differentiation is how I explain the purpose of art and that what we do is not to be standardized. The purpose is that we all see art through a different lens which, in turn, creates an interpretation. We then listen to a piece of music, and I ask them what they notice. These simple exercises get them thinking, and as a result, they are more willing to share their ideas and be expressive in their performance.

Words of Wisdom
Gleason challenges himself and other teachers to think globally about the value of music education:

As music teachers, I think it is not enough to play a great piece of music well. I think we as educators have more to teach our students. My goal is for my students to be more curious every day. Young children ask so many questions, but by the time they get to high school, they become disengaged and not as curious. Teachers have to keep asking questions so that students leave school being more mindful about life and society. Teaching is a complex, ever-evolving skill, but our goal should be to a light a fire in kids to keep learning so they can succeed beyond their wildest dreams.

Corey Graves

"Slow and steady wins the race."

Corey Graves is currently the director of bands at Roma Middle School in Roma, Texas. He is a Bill and Melinda Gates Millennium Scholar and received his bachelor of music education degree summa cum laude from Stephen F. Austin State University. He also earned a master of music in euphonium performance from The Ohio State University.

Program Structure

After graduating from The Ohio State University, Corey Graves moved to the Rio Grande Valley and began his teaching career as a tuba and euphonium teacher at Palmview High School in La Joya Independent School District (ISD). After one year, he became director of bands at Lorenzo de Zavala Middle School and the following year, moved to Roma ISD as director of bands at Roma Middle School. Roma Middle School has more than 750 students enrolled in grades six through eight, with 260 students participating in band. Graves is one of twelve band directors in Roma ISD, each of whom specializes in a different instrument. There are six directors at Roma High School, three directors at Roma Middle School, and three directors at Ramiro Barrera Middle School. All twelve directors teach at Roma High School in the morning, then teach the beginning band classes and assist with the three concert bands at Roma Middle School, and end their day teaching at Ramiro Barrera Middle School. Each class meets for forty-five minutes. He explained that teamwork is critical to this structure:

We are a rurally located, Title I school district, and access to private lesson teachers and resources is limited. However, there is tremendous support for fine arts. For our students to have the tools to be successful and competitive in the state, we hire directors who specialize in a specific instrument to supplement the student's learning. It is a team effort, and if one person fails, we all fail. However, if everybody is philosophically aligned and works hard for the students, we will all be successful. We are fortunate to have a fantastic staff who understand the expectations and take pride in what they do to create an exceptional experience for our students. It is a unique situation, but the best part is that we see our students over seven years—from the first day of sixth grade to their high school graduation.

Graves opens the band hall each morning at 6:30 a.m., and sectionals occur before and after school. Graves teaches sectionals for the top ensemble, symphonic winds, and holds a full band rehearsal every Friday after school. "Sectionals are your opportunity to teach instrument-specific techniques and exercises as well as address instrument-specific issues from the full band rehearsal," he said. "This is where you build relationships with the students, where they get to know you, and where you come to understand who they are and how they learn on a deeper level."

All seventh and eighth-grade band students perform a fall, winter, and spring concert as well as a pre-contest concert. They also perform at the region contest and at three or four regional festivals at local universities and performance halls. During the first semester, students in the top ensemble are required to audition for the all-region band. Students in the second and third bands who have met the audition standard will also audition for the all-region band. For the audition, students prepare three etudes, seven major scales, and a chromatic scale. "We focus heavily on the individual at the beginning of the year through the all-region process," Graves said. "These experiences make the students better in the full ensemble setting, and they are more prepared to play advanced literature during the second semester." Students also participate in a solo and ensemble festival in April and attend instrument-specific workshops with guest performers and clinicians throughout the year.

Instrumentation
At the end of the school year, students audition for one of the three concert bands. They have seven minutes to perform an etude, major scales, and a

chromatic scale, as well as demonstrate their rhythmic and sight-reading ability. Seventh graders in the top ensemble play all twelve major scales, and students in the second ensemble play seven major scales. Beginning band students play the scales they know and an excerpt of music they can perform at a high level. "We want the audition process to demonstrate what each student has learned throughout the year and how they have grown as a musician," Graves said. "Therefore, the requirements change with each ensemble and grade level." Graves administers each audition, and he records each one so the other band directors can also assess the progress of the student and create goals for the following year.

Graves places students in an ensemble that is appropriate for their development. "We must facilitate the high school program with quality players so it is important to place them in an ensemble where they can develop the skills they need," he said. The top ensemble typically has six to eight flutes, one or two oboes, two bassoons, eight to ten clarinets, two bass clarinets, three to four alto saxophones, one tenor saxophone, one baritone saxophone, six to eight trumpets, six to eight horns, five or six trombones, three or four euphoniums, three or four tubas, and seven to eight percussionists.

Graves' ensemble setup changes each year, depending on the strengths and weaknesses of the ensemble and the music the ensemble is performing. He often places the first parts in the center of the ensemble and the second and third parts near the end of the row to create a more equal balance. This setup also allows the section leaders to listen to and balance with one another. The trumpets are on a low riser in the center of the ensemble, and the trombones sit directly behind the trumpets on a higher riser. "I have found that with risers, middle school brass players do not have to play excessively loud and distort their sound in order to be heard," he said. "However, you must rehearse with them from the beginning of the rehearsal process so the ensemble can adjust to the sound."

Recruitment
There are six elementary schools in Roma ISD and three of them feed into Roma Middle School. There is no elementary music program in the district, and many students are first-generation band students. "It is the first time many of these students have been part of a large ensemble, so we must constantly educate and make the students and parents aware of what they will experience as a member of the band," Graves said.

In December, the top ensemble performs a holiday concert at each elementary school. Once a week in March, Graves briefly visits each fifth-grade classroom to promote the band. "I have learned that students are more likely to sign up if you make your presence known on campus, if you are friendly, and if they can see your personality early on," he said. "I tell students that the band is the largest organization on campus, band students are the best students to be around, and they will already have an eighth-grade big brother or sister when they start middle school if they join the band."

There is an assembly for the fifth-grade class at each elementary school, in which the symphonic winds perform several pop music charts and Graves showcases each instrument. Graves makes the assembly interactive and uses it as an opportunity to teach performance etiquette. "We teach the fifth graders how to behave in a concert as well as when and how to clap," said Graves. "We also give them a list of the instruments, and they describe the sounds of each of the instrument, circling their favorites." After the concert, each student receives an informational letter to give to their parents and a teacher recommendation form.

Shortly after the assembly, fifth graders are invited to attend a "band night" on two evenings during the week. Roma High School hosts the event as it is the most central location for the parent community. Prospective students meet all of the band directors, see and play all of the instruments, and choose which instrument they would like to play. Students also return the teacher recommendation form, which provides insight into the student's personality. Graves said:

> We take every kid that wants to be in the band program. However, we want to know who the class leaders are, who the independent workers are, which students prefer to work in groups, which students are the troublemakers, which students are responsible and diligent, which students excel in class, or which students need assistance. If I know how a student behaves, I can pair him or her with a specific teacher that will be a good fit in beginning band.

In addition to the student's personality, Graves assesses the student's physical characteristics to place him or her on the right instrument. He avoids placing students on flute, trumpet, or French horn who have a prominent teardrop in their top lip. Flute players are typically confident and detailed students, while double reed players are extroverted, academic, and independent students. Additionally, Graves avoids placing students on a woodwind instrument if they are double jointed. Students interested in clarinet need to be able to form a firm, flat chin and have a well-aligned bite. Students with thin to medium lips are better served on trumpet and French horn, while students with medium to full lips are encouraged to play a low brass instrument. Future percussionists must have a strong internal pulse and advanced fine motor skills. Finally, for students interested in double reeds, French horn, or trombone, Graves will often use a music aptitude test to assess the student's inner ear.

Beginning Band Curriculum

Graves typically has 100–120 beginners each year. The school district provides oboes, bassoons, French horns, trombones, euphoniums, tubas, and percussion, and the beginning band instrumentation is based on the availability of instruments and the needs of the student. Since there are no elementary music programs in Roma ISD, the first week is devoted to music theory and establishing the expectations and procedures for rehearsal. Graves said:

> Students learn the proper way to enter the classroom on the first day of school. We line everybody up outside of the band hall, each student stands on a square tile directly behind their neighbor and quietly enters. We introduce all of the band directors, and students learn where to place their backpack. We also teach them how to sit in their assigned chair with a call and response chant: "Feet flat on the floor, rump on the bump, sit tall, hold still."

Once Graves establishes the procedure, students demonstrate their understanding by teaching Graves how to enter the room and assume the correct posture for rehearsal.

Each studio teacher is responsible for teaching playing posture, hand position, embouchure, and breathing techniques for their specific instrument. Beginners do not use a method book initially because Graves wants to teach fundamental skills that can then be applied later to songs. Exercises specific to each instrument are therefore written by each studio teacher. These exercises build a characteristic tone quality and facility on the instrument and include simple lip and register slurs, technical exercises, and articulation drills.

Beginning band students are assessed through weekly playing tests. Students receive a check-plus, check, or check-minus for their performance. Those that receive a check-plus are considered "first chair," students who earn a check are "second chair," and students who earn a check-minus are "third chair." The following week, students sit in groups based on their chair placement. "In this system, I do not have to tell any student that they are the last chair," Graves said. "However, they are still held accountable and given specific information on how to improve the following week."

Repertoire Selection

When choosing repertoire, Graves balances the concepts and skills his students need to develop and the compositions he wants his students to play and experience. He believes it is crucial for students to perform as many different types of music as possible. "It is easy for directors to like one type of music and only teach one type of music," said Graves. "However, we have to ask ourselves what our students need for their musical education, what the ensemble needs, and what the ensemble is capable of playing." Each year, Graves will perform at least one multi-movement work because it requires maturity and endurance and teaches students about thematic development. Each band will also play works of various cultures, a march to help teach style and articulation, a lyrical piece that strengthens the student's musical maturity, music by living composers, pop music, show tunes, or movie soundtracks that are relatable to the student, and works that feature the percussion section.

At the beginning of the year, Graves plans his repertoire with the end-goal in mind. He said:

> I choose several pieces I think the ensemble can play by the end of the year and find easier music to play in the first semester that develops those concepts. For example, if I know what march I am going to play in April, I will choose an easier one to play at the beginning of the year. The fall concert is a great time to build the weaker sections. At the end of the year, I try to choose music that highlights individual players and the strengths of the ensemble, while also providing challenges for every student.

Score Study and Rehearsal Planning

"Don't dare walk into a rehearsal without a plan," Graves said. "If students figure out that you did not prepare, you make it acceptable for them not to

80

prepare." Before rehearsal, Graves spends many hours studying the score, sometimes learning it so well that he does not even need to use the score in rehearsal. He highlights the melody in yellow, countermelodies in green and purple, and the bass line in orange. As a visual learner, the colors allow Graves to understand and quickly reference the orchestration. He listens to numerous recordings by professional, collegiate, and middle school bands in order to understand the standard and overall goal of the piece. In particular, live recordings, both good and bad, of other middle schools playing the same piece help give him a realistic understanding of the challenges ahead. He extracts the concepts that students will need to learn and makes a detailed plan for teaching them in sectionals. "I never teach anything in the full band rehearsal unless I have taught it in a sectional first," he said. "In the ensemble rehearsal, I want students to focus on putting the music together and learning how their part fits within the entire piece."

Each rehearsal at Roma begins with the "daily drill," a series of warmup exercises designed to improve the individual and ensemble fundamentals. Early in the year, Graves spends a significant amount of time on the daily drill in order to master the exercises. As the concert approaches, more time is spent on the music, but the daily drill is adapted to address the ongoing challenges in the repertoire. "If I have taught the fundamentals correctly and adapted the daily drill to address the challenges in the music, the music should come together fairly quickly," he said. "For example, if there is a difficult rhythm in compound meter in the music, the students perform the daily drill on that rhythm and we add different dynamics and articulations depending on the needs of the ensemble."

Overall, Graves believes that a great rehearsal consists of giving concise, accurate information with as few words as possible and having a detailed plan for how to fix what is wrong. He said:

> If I am taking more than four beats to talk, it is too much; I have lost the attention and engagement of my students. Many teachers want to explain everything on the podium, but nothing gets better as a result. Quick bursts of specific information create the most productive rehearsals.

Tone
When teaching students to play with a characteristic tone, Graves plays numerous recordings that demonstrate both good and bad tone qualities.

Students must also explain why the tone quality is right or what is creating the poor tone quality. "Students need to be able to hear and fix a poor tone quality to be mature, independent musicians," he said. "I think directors often put too much pressure on themselves to fix everything when, in reality, we can teach students to be aware and hold them accountable for correcting the issues on their own."

Rehearsals begin by establishing a proper posture and performing a series of breathing exercises. Students hold their hands vertical to their mouths and breathe in and out for a set amount of counts. They also extend the hand away from the mouth to sustain the speed and movement of air. "We talk about engaging the 'tummy' and making the body fat with air, then making it skinny," Graves said. "Breathing exercises also focus the students for rehearsal after coming from different classes."

To help establish a proper embouchure in the first semester, Graves and his staff use mirrors, so that students can see whether they are consistently placing the mouthpiece in the correct position. Breathing exercises, posture, and embouchure placement are reinforced in the daily drill with Remington exercises, lip and register slurs, and Cichowicz Flow Studies, with the goal of developing an extended range and a mature tone quality. "We build range based on what was done the day before," he said. "The student will be successful if the director works slowly and methodically to ensure that they are set up correctly with equipment that is in proper working condition."

Intonation

"You cannot tune a bad tone quality," Graves said. "However, if students have a great sound and are using their air properly, they can learn to adjust their instruments." In beginning band, Graves teaches students to hum first so they become comfortable and confident with the vibrations and they are creating. "Singing can be uncomfortable for naturally shy students and for boys whose voices are changing," Graves said. "To make them more comfortable, I first ask my students to hum loud enough to feel the buzz in their nose. When they gain confidence, we open up the mouth and sing." Students hum, sing, and play an exercise or excerpt of music to match the vocal quality and pitch on their instrument. Graves also asks students to match pitch to a drone. Using a Yamaha Harmony Director, Graves will adjust the pitch to A440, A442, A438, or A444. He teaches students how to make the necessary adjustments to match the drone until they can accomplish the task on their own.

Part of the daily drill includes an exercise called "passing eights." This exercise begins with the full ensemble, then the tubas, and continues in reverse score order. Each section sustains one pitch for eight counts and passes it to the next section. The purpose is to match intonation and tone quality, but the exercise can also address dynamics, sustains, starts, and releases. Graves also assigns students into mini-bands at the beginning of the year. Adopted by Texas middle school band director Melodianne Mallow, Graves creates small ensembles of soprano, alto, tenor, and bass voices and places strong players with weak players. In rehearsal, Graves will have one or multiple mini-bands play a particular chord or excerpt of music and adjust the intonation, balance, or clarity. "Mini-bands provide a leadership experience for our stronger players and a learning experience for the weaker players," added Graves. "It holds students more accountable for their part and as a result, there is a more unified ensemble sound."

Rhythm

During the first week of class, Graves uses pop music to teach students about rhythm and pulse. He will play a pop song and have students count to four while clapping on the first beat, stomping on the second beat, standing up on the third beat, and sitting down on the fourth beat. They repeat the sequence over multiple repetitions, and Graves includes different variations, movements, and tempos to teach students to internalize pulse. "I try to find activities that not only teach them about rhythm and keeping a steady pulse but gets them out of their chair and expends built-up energy."

Graves uses the Eastman system of counting because it reinforces articulation using the tip of the tongue. As students learn new rhythms, they always write in the counts and count the rhythm out loud while tapping their foot. "Having students tap their foot allows me to see how coordinated they are and assess their ability to maintain a steady pulse," said Graves. "Some students do not have that ability, so we do not allow them to tap their foot because it gets in the way of their development."

When students are learning to read rhythms using a rhythm chart, Graves will play a game called "Don't Drop the Baby." He explained:

Every student is responsible for counting one measure of the rhythm chart with a metronome. I do not always start at measure 1 because kids will plan, in advance, which measure they have to count based on their assigned seat. If one student makes a mistake, everybody has to start over. I also start with a different student each time, especially if a student is struggling with a particular measure. Once the class can successfully count the rhythmic pattern, students count one beat of one measure with a metronome. This activity maintains engagement and focus, while also holding them accountable.

Graves also created the "Box of Happiness, Joy, and Smiles" as a way of holding students accountable and practicing performing for their peers. Each student's name is put into an empty box three times. "If their name is only in the box once, the student will not practice after their first performance," he said. On any given day, Graves will draw a name out of the box, and the student has to count a particular rhythm or play a certain exercise or excerpt of music. "I never choose anything they should not know already, and we use it as a way to encourage and push students, not to threaten or embarrass them in front of their peers."

Technique

In beginning band, Graves and his staff teach students to hold the instrument with a natural hand position that is free of tension. Once they have developed a fundamental tone quality and learned to articulate, Graves introduces scales using tetrachords. "Students need to understand how to build a scale before they can play it," he said. Students learn the first tetrachord of a scale, followed by the second tetrachord, and then the entire scale. Graves also rewrote the first three exercises of the Clarke Studies, in quarter notes, in different ranges so that beginners of all levels can perform them. He explained the value of these exercises:

These exercises not only teach students to play in the key signature but help students, especially brass players, understand pitch relationships, because the partials are close together. Clarke Studies also provide a technical challenge for the low voices and allow those students to develop the same skill and dexterity as the flute players.

To encourage technical development, Graves began a program called "Scale Star," which challenges students to pass-off their scales for another member of the Roma ISD band staff. If a student can play seven major scales at 120 BPM plus a chromatic scale at 88 BPM with zero mistakes, a star with their name on it is posted in the band hall. "We are very strict about who passes because we want to build confidence in their ability to perform," he said. "The students also take enormous pride in seeing their name on the wall." Students can reach the second level of "Scale Star" by playing all of their major scales plus their chromatic scale. Playing their natural, harmonic, and melodic minor scales allows them to reach the fourth and fifth level. Finally, students can reach the sixth level if they play every scale with only three mistakes. "We have had several students that were very motivated and talented reach the sixth level, and those students have helped set the standard and push their peers to be better."

Balance and Blend

When teaching the concepts of balance and blend, Graves will often show his students his highlighted score, which indicates the melody, counter-melodies, and bass accompaniment. "It is important to ask questions and guide students' ears in rehearsal," he said. "Can they hear their neighbor? Are they supporting or dominating the melodic line? What is their level of importance in the music?" Students write their melodic priority in the music or identify which instruments have the main melodic line. Depending on the work the ensemble is performing, Graves will then rewrite the dynamics or orchestration to create more transparency, clarity, and depth. He said:

> Composers did not write many grade-4 works for a middle school ensemble, and the composer did not write the piece for my band or my students. I will rewrite an individual part if a particular student is struggling with the technique or if I am unable to fix the intonation or balance. I will redistribute parts of the chord if there is a lack of transparency or the chord has too much bass or soprano. I try to keep the integrity of the composer's intention, but also want to create the best overall product for my students.

In the daily drill, Graves uses five "color groups" to teach students how woodwind and brass instruments blend to create new timbres. Also taken from Melodianne Mallow, the first group consists of flute, oboe, and trumpet; the second group is horn and clarinet; the third group is alto saxophone and trombones; the fourth group is bassoon, tenor saxophone, and euphonium; and the fifth group is bass clarinet, baritone saxophone, and tuba. In rehearsal, Graves will have the fourth and fifth groups play a particular passage, adjust the balance and blend, and then add the other three groups to create a more vibrant and warmer ensemble sound. Graves also modifies the instruments within each group based on the orchestration of the music. "The color groups typically correspond to who has the melody, counter-melody, and bass accompaniment in the repertoire," Graves said. "We can create better transparency and clarity by isolating each group and allowing students to hear and adjust to one another."

Musicianship
"In sixth grade, I think we often get caught up in teaching half notes and quarter notes but lose sight of the music," said Graves. "We always sing the music we are playing and then transfer the vocal quality to the instruments, moving the air to shape the phrase." Graves believes in giving students the tools to be great musicians, making them responsible for their music-making, and allowing time for students to experiment with their ideas. He said:

> We encourage students to take liberties within the music and teach them, for example, where to add vibrato or why specific notes should be elongated within a phrase or before a rest. When they are preparing their solos and all-region etudes, they will perform for one another, and we will discuss the choices that they made and why they did or did not work. It is essential to teach students, from the very beginning, that making music is about doing more than what is on the page.

Words of Wisdom
"Your attitude determines your altitude," Graves said. "If you have a positive attitude and a game plan for achieving your goals, you will be successful. If Plan A does not work out, there are twenty-five more letters in the alphabet." Graves frequently records his rehearsals and solicits opinions from his friends, colleagues, and mentors. He also plays the recordings for his ensemble. "What we hear and perceive in our inner ear is often different than the reality of what is happening," he said. "It is important to receive multiple opinions from trusted colleagues and mentors to challenge what and how we hear."

More importantly, Graves believes it is vital that teachers show students how much they care:

Kids know when you are disingenuous. They may be young, but they are not dumb. I do not sell my kids short or lower my expectations for any reason. Kids are kids and no matter who they are or where they are from, they still miss A-natural and F-sharp. Students can always do more than we give them credit for, and it is our job to create a culture that gives them the skills to be not just a better musician but a better person.

Robert Herrings

"It's expectation with love."

Robert Herrings is currently the director of bands at Artie Henry Middle School in Cedar Park, Texas. He earned his bachelor's degree in music education from Baylor University.

Program Structure

After two years as the assistant director at Artie Henry Middle School in Leander Independent School District (ISD), Robert Herrings was promoted to director of bands in 2006. The school opened in 2002 and currently has an enrollment of approximately 1,300 students in grades six through eight. Approximately 350 students participate in band. Herrings has two assistants, with additional instruction provided by a full-time percussion instructor. Fine arts programs in Leander ISD receive substantial support thanks to Ron Morrison, the former fine arts supervisor, who fought for specialized instruction in the elementary and middle school programs. Herrings said:

> Ron was adamant about showing administrators that in no other class is there a 1:60 ratio. He would use the analogy that we would never teach math and science in the same class, so why would we teach flute and oboe in the same class? The superintendent at the time was a theater teacher with children in the band, so he understood and supported the fine arts programs. Our current superintendent has continued this support because of the successes we have had. It takes time, but we have had incredible support from the top down in a community that sees the value of arts education.

Seventh and eighth-grade students are divided into three concert bands and beginning band students are divided into three blocks of homogeneous classes. Each class meets daily and lasts between forty-six and fifty-two minutes. The band hall opens daily at 6:30 a. m., and the directors begin sectionals for all three concert bands at 7:30 a.m. These last one hour and fifteen minutes and also occur after school until 5:30 p.m. Herrings firmly believes that the most effective and detailed teaching happens in sectionals, because students receive individual, specific attention and build meaningful relationships with their fellow section members. Also, sectionals are where new music can be introduced so that ensemble rehearsals can address larger concepts aimed at the collective whole.

When the top ensemble, the honors band, was first selected to perform at the Midwest Clinic in 2010, Herrings began after-school rehearsals on Friday afternoons leading up to the concert:

> These rehearsals were so effective because we did not have to spend time on announcements or fundamentals. There were no after-school athletics or in-class lessons, so it was the only opportunity to have the full ensemble present. We now do these rehearsals all year, and my kids look forward to it. We get a lot accomplished and make it as fun as possible. Different families bring snacks each week, and afterward we have Friday dance parties.

The concert bands perform six concerts per year: a fall, winter, and spring concert, as well as a pre-contest concert, contest, and a spring trip or festival performance. Beginning band students perform at the winter and spring concerts. During the first semester, students in the top ensemble and those studying privately are required to audition for the all-region band. Students must prepare three high-quality etudes for their audition, and Herrings believes that these etudes, selected by the district band directors, help teach, develop, and reinforce fundamental skills and further enrich the student's education. When preparing students for the audition, Herrings divides the etudes into sections, and gives the students bronze, silver, and gold performance tempos. The students work on their music both individually and in sectionals, perform often for their peers, and send recordings to Herrings and his staff for feedback. The entire process is designed to build confidence in the student's individual musicianship and improve each student's contribution to the ensemble setting.

In early February, students in the top two bands participate in an ensemble contest, and in May, all students, including beginners, perform solos as part of a district-wide contest. The directors choose challenging pieces that demonstrate what students have learned throughout the year while also pushing them to the next level.

Private Lessons

When Herrings first arrived at Henry, a stigma surrounded private lessons, because they were presented as tutoring rather than enrichment. When he became director of bands, he encouraged private lessons as a tool for success and provided students with numerous instrument-specific teacher options so that they could find the best fit. Participation soared once the enrolled students became successful, and Herrings never had to make private lessons a requirement. Seventy percent of the students are currently enrolled in private lessons, and Leander ISD offers financial aid to students who qualify. At times, Herrings has personally donated his own money to help dedicated, motivated students. He said:

> If a kid is working hard for me, I do whatever I can to help. Our job is to give students all of the tools possible to be successful, and that may or may not include private lessons. I grew up with a single mom who did everything she could to make sure we had what we needed. I want my students to have the same opportunity, and I do whatever I can to make band a worthwhile experience.

For those students who are not able to take private lessons, Herrings and his colleagues offer guidance and detailed feedback after school, on the weekends, or through recorded listening exams.

Instrumentation

When he became director of bands, Herrings' priority was to restructure the curriculum to ensure vertical alignment from the beginner classes through the concert ensembles. Herrings typically limits the number of students in the top ensemble because of the musical demand and pace of rehearsals. The top ensemble usually consists of seven flutes, three oboes, eleven clarinets, three bassoons, two bass clarinets, three or four alto saxophones, one or two tenor saxophones, one baritone saxophone, six French horns, six to eight trumpets, six trombones, three euphoniums, four tubas, and six to eight percussionists.

"The second band should be the training ensemble and the heart of every program," Herrings said. Therefore, he places more students in this ensemble because, with less difficult literature, enrichment and fundamental training can be the primary focus and students are better prepared for the rigor of the top ensemble. Additionally, students who would be placed towards the bottom of the second band are instead given leadership opportunities in the third band. They act as mentors and role models to other students in the ensemble. "We always want to make students in the second and third band feel valued and important and provide them with constant motivation to practice and improve," he said.

Recruitment

Herrings firmly believes every student needs to find an artistic outlet for their individuality, whether it be singing, dancing, theater, art, orchestra, or band, and he strives to attract the right type of students to band. "Band students are those that have a strong work ethic, understand challenges and delayed gratification, and display a desire to grow and learn," he said. Herrings noted the difficult transition from the innocence of elementary school to the more structured routine of middle school:

> Middle school is the first time many students experience failure. We tell beginning band parents early on that they should expect their child to get a failing grade on their first whole-note test because it is going to be incorrect. However, they have limitless opportunities to retest, and we are always striving for continuous improvement. This concept of delayed gratification is challenging for many perfectionist students and parents to grasp initially. We want students that are willing to be vulnerable and keep learning after failing. All kids are great kids, and I will always give every student an opportunity to be in the band, but there comes the point where we determine whether the student is going to be successful and have an exceptional experience in our program. It's okay if band is not the right fit or if they do not want to be in the band; some students would instead sing, dance, or act.

Herrings recruits students from five elementary schools. In December, the band and choir (there is currently no orchestra program in the school district) perform a holiday concert for each of the elementary schools. An informational brochure is sent to every elementary school student following the concert that outlines the fine arts opportunities at Henry. Herrings then holds a "meet the instruments" night for students and parents, in which the private lesson staff and local teachers demonstrate each of the instruments and distribute more specific information about the program. In the spring, the honors band will play for the fifth graders during a tour of Henry Middle School. Students from each section play a recognizable tune linked by a drumbeat.

Overall, Herrings believes that increased visibility and being involved in the community will attract students to the band program. Similarly, directors have to continuously educate parents on what happens in their program. Herrings said:

> Parents are also a vital component of the recruitment process. They tell their friends to put their child in the band because of what they will learn and experience. They tell other parents their child will be surrounded by the best kids and the right kids in the school. Prospective parents hesitate because there is a cost, but once they realize the quality of education their child will receive, recognize that we have financial aid, and compare it to other programs in the school, they want their child to be involved. This reputation took five or six years to develop, but now the machine continues to run itself, as long as we keep doing our jobs.

Beginning Band Setup

Around 150 students typically enroll in beginning band at Henry. For Herrings, anything more than this becomes unmanageable. Although he wants to give every student the opportunity to be in the band, he is mindful that as the student to teacher ratio climbs, individual instruction suffers:

> The more students enrolled, the less attention they will receive and more unsuccessful they will be which, in the end, affects their overall experience. I believe that if you hire a math teacher on your campus, you want that teacher to teach math correctly. Therefore, when you hire a band director, it should be the expectation that the band director teaches the flute player how to play their flute correctly and the clarinet player how to play the clarinet correctly. Sometimes we have a double standard with elective teachers that it should just be fun. We have a lot of fun at Henry, but just like the math teacher, we strive to teach them how to play their instruments correctly.

Herrings and his coworkers teach three blocks of homogenous beginner classes. The first block is flute, saxophone, and French horn. The second block is clarinet, trombone, and percussion, and the third block is trumpet, double reeds, and tuba/euphonium. Homogeneous classes provide detailed, individual instruction for beginning students, yet several challenges remain. At the beginning of the year, every student is at the same level. In December, the class has a small bell curve, and by March, the classes have typically split into advanced, intermediate, and beginning level. More advanced students can participate in an audition-based "select band," which meets once a week after school during the second semester. This ensemble helps keep them challenged and engaged with advanced fundamental skills, basic ensemble skills, and grade 2 concert literature. Advanced seventh and eighth-grade students also act as mentors, leading sectionals or participating in ensemble rehearsals.

Herrings continues to pay attention to those beginners who struggle, because often they form the core of the band. He said:

> The bottom of the class is challenging. Early in my career, I forgot about those students, but then I started to realize that the quality of the program is in the second and third bands. Those are the kids that want to be there and will continue to be in high school band, whereas many of the kids in the top band often excel at many other activities and are more likely to quit. Some of the best high school players come from the third middle school band because everybody learns at a different pace. I always teach to the middle of the class because if they are the right type of kid, it is my job to find a way of delivering information so the light bulb clicks.

Herrings distributes a list of recommended instruments to all beginning band families, and if a family wants to deviate, Herrings or his assistants must approve. Herrings frequently communicates with local music stores and parents to ensure that beginning students receive proper instruments. "For that child to be successful, they must play on a quality instrument," he said. "We work with music stores to make it affordable for our families."

For the intermediate and advanced beginners, Herrings and his colleagues encourage the purchase of step-up instruments towards the end of sixth grade or beginning of seventh grade. He provides students with several brands and models to consider. Local music stores will often visit the sectional classes or after-school rehearsals and work with families to offer a long-term, no-interest financial plan. To educate and convince parents of the investment, Herrings will equate purchasing a step-up instrument to buying a new pair of shoes:

> Parents typically have to buy a new pair of shoes for their child at the end of the sixth and seventh grade. I sell it as if they can buy one pair of shoes that will last them through college. We can't require our parents to purchase step-up instruments, but if the students are serious about music, we discuss the long-term investment and the success the student will have.

Beginning Band Curriculum

Herrings' primary goal in beginning band is to teach students a detailed, fundamental approach to playing their instrument, rather than focusing on how far they progress through their method books. By the end of the first year, he works to ensure that students have:

- proper posture, hand position, and embouchure placement
- a characteristic tone quality across a wide range
- a thorough knowledge of how the instrument functions
- solid foundation of rhythm, technique, and articulation
- an ability to comprehend music and translate it to their instrument
- an understanding of how to practice effectively

Herrings uses a wide array of method books and supplemental materials, and the accomplishments of the previous day determine the pace. He said:

> When teaching band, especially beginners, everything builds on the day before and the skills developed in the last lesson. Directors can never forget that these students are blank canvases. They have no set concept or idea of what band is so what we tell them is all they know. This is why we place an enormous emphasis on the small stuff—how they enter the room, proper behavior, their posture, their hand position, and their embouchure—from the very beginning. If you set that expectation from the first day and reinforce those elements on a daily basis, everything along the way will be more successful.

Beginning band students are assessed through three playing tests every six weeks, with limitless opportunities to retest. Students play one at a time in front of their peers, to build confidence performing for an audience. "Everybody claps after each student's performance because we teach our students that the goal is to build each other up, not tear each other down," he said.

Following the exam, Herrings will only announce the top five scores on the playing exams. He also gives awards for best hand position, best embouchure, best posture, best tone, best pulse, or any other category that can help reward multiple students for their effort and improvement. "We try to build comradery and support for one another in the section in a healthy and fun way," he said. "In the process, we hope the students will motivate one another."

Herrings does not grade the students during the exams. Instead, playing tests are videotaped and graded that evening. Students are given a rubric with handwritten comments, and if they would like to retest, they bring in the previous rubric and demonstrate what aspects have improved. These videos can then be used to show parents the student's progress or note areas for improvement if there are concerns. After a period of time, Herrings erases the videos.

Herrings advises directors to give beginning band students only the information they need. "Keep it short, concise, and to the point, and keep them playing as much as possible," he said. Learning activities vary between breathing and singing exercises, playing long tones and articulation exercises on the mouthpiece or head joint, technical exercises on the middle parts of the instrument, note naming and rhythm games, and theory packets. Genuine feedback, either positive or negative, is always provided after each repetition. Herrings added:

> You continuously have to dangle the carrot to keep them practicing and progressing. For example, we encourage students to practice their embouchure so they can take their mouthpiece home. Then we encourage them to practice on their mouthpiece so they can take their instrument home and learn their first songs. Each day builds on the next, every day is fun, and we always celebrate the small victories, so they leave excited and desiring more.

Score Study and Rehearsal Preparation
When first learning a score, Herrings listens to numerous recordings of a piece to formulate an informed, interpretive aural image of the work. "I want my students to feel like I know the score and can teach it at the very highest level," he said. He then uses colored highlighters to mark the melody, countermelody, and accompaniment for easier identification

in rehearsal. He analyzes all harmonic cadences and instrument ranges, looking for potential difficulties in technique, intonation, articulation, and rhythm. From there, Herrings develops a detailed plan for how and when to teach those problematic concepts.

Understanding the historical aspects of the piece and the reason or inspiration for the composition is also essential. For major works on a concert, Herrings shares the story or significance to inform the student's performance. He said:

> Every year, we play "America the Beautiful" for Veterans Day, and I take time to discuss the origin and history of this piece. The students might have heard it before but never understood its meaning or significance. We need to take time to do that, especially at the beginning of their musical careers. I try to do this with every significant piece we perform.

Tone

Over the years, Herrings has developed his order of priorities for student development and ensemble progress, referred to as his "Sweet T.A.R.T.S"—Tone, Articulation, Rhythm, Technique, and Style. Tone quality is the most important priority for Herrings and his staff. "If it is not a characteristic tone that sounds like the instrument, nothing else matters," he said. At the beginning of the year, students spend a significant amount of time with their mouthpieces to ensure that their embouchure is set correctly before assembling the instrument. Herrings collects the mouthpieces at the end of each class, so that incorrect habits do not develop at home. Once embouchure and posture are correct, students begin tone development exercises on the mouthpiece or head joint. During this time, they are also learning how to put the instrument together, practicing proper hand position, and performing silent exercises that reinforce technical coordination and dexterity. After a few weeks, students begin playing on their instruments. His approach is intentionally methodical to build a solid foundation. He said:

> Many people think we work too slowly with our beginners, but many students are unsuccessful in high school because they did not correctly learn a specific fundamental skill at the beginning. These fundamental skills are an ongoing process, and directors can never forget that it is easier to set them up correctly than change it later.

Articulation and Style

Herrings introduces articulation when most students are playing with a full, characteristic tone. Every beginner class and concert ensemble plays the same articulation exercise every day: a whole note, two connected half notes, four connected quarter notes, four lifted quarter notes, four separated quarter notes, eight connected eighth notes, eight lifted eighth notes, twelve connected triplets, and twelve lifted triplets. A breakdown of sixteenth notes follows, in which students play one sixteenth note on each beat, followed by two sixteenth notes, three sixteenth notes, and finally four beats of continuous sixteenth notes. Students then play four sixteenth notes plus one note and eight sixteenth notes plus one note, to work on forward direction of the air across the beat.

In sectionals, Herrings will have students play this exercise without using the tongue, starting notes with only their air. "The speed of air drives articulation," he said. "If students can get an immediate, fundamental sound with just their air, the tongue will add clarity if it knows where to touch."

To create a clear and consistent articulation, Herrings continually addresses tongue placement. If single-reed players are articulating too low on the reed or using the middle part of the tongue to articulate, Herrings places a dot on the center of the tip of the reed using a wet-erase transparency marker. Students will articulate a few times, look in a mirror, and see where they are articulating. If the black dot is on the top of their tongue, it is correct; if there is no dot, the student is articulating too low. Brass players buzz daily to hear the connection or separation of air between notes. With horn players, Herrings uses the phrase, "touch the tip of the tongue to the top of the tooth," or has students think the words "tho" or "thuh" to lower the tongue position. Herrings summarized:

> Each instrument has specifics for proper articulation. Our job is to learn what those are, find the individuals not doing it exactly as we want it, give them detailed information to fix it, and hold them accountable for doing it the same way every time they play.

Intonation

Although students frequently sing in elementary music classes, beginning band students learn to sing during the first week. In fact, the choir director at Henry will teach the introductory lesson on proper singing technique to all beginning classes. Fundamental exercises ranging from one note to chorales, Remington exercises, Cichowicz Flow Studies, Clarke Studies, and specific musical passages are sung daily. Over three years, both intonation and tone quality drastically improve. Herrings said:

> With singing, you have to educate the students on the benefits, and if you are excited and encouraging about it, they will comply. We always start with humming, telling the students that their noses should tickle like a bumble bee. We then ask them to drop their jaw into an "ah" sound. From there, we try to refine the pitch and then match it on our instruments so our tone quality emulates the voice.

During the second semester of sixth grade, students use clip-on tuners to refine pitch awareness. In seventh grade, clip-on tuners are only used as a reference during ensemble fundamentals or to tune complex chords. Herrings also frequently uses a Yamaha Harmony Director to demonstrate the difference between equal and just intonation. He said:

> Kids are smarter than directors give them credit for, and kids know when it sounds right and wrong, even in sixth grade. If we allow them, they can tweak intonation issues on their own, but only if we develop their inner ear from the very beginning and teach them what is right and what is wrong.

Rhythm

Beginning band students at Henry have a basic understanding of the rhythmic structure and time signatures from their elementary school music classes. Over time, the elementary teachers have adopted the same counting system used by Herrings and his assistants. To distinguish between sustained notes and quicker rhythmic values, students will say "dash" between larger beats. For example, students chant, "1-dash-2-dash-3-dash-4" when counting a whole note. Rather than saying "dash" on the last eighth note, students will pulse or slightly raise their voices on "4" to emphasize the change and reinforce the upbeat. When eighth notes are introduced, students will then count "1-and-2-and-3-and-4-and" and pulse the last eighth note. Students count sixteenth notes "1-e-and-uh," and compound meter is taught using "1-la-lee." Before playing, students will always count the line of music while tapping their foot with a metronome. As students advance, students clap where they should articulate or finger/position, repeating the exercise until they do not make any mistakes. Herrings described the importance of the metronome to all levels of players:

> Students must use a metronome because they need a stable pulse to build their skills. College and professional musicians always practice with a metronome, and it is our job to instill those habits in our students. No matter the level, there needs to be a vertical alignment to play musically. The musicianship will never be realized if the vertical alignment is not correct.

Technique

Before beginning band, sixth-grade students have learned to read notes on the staff, have a rudimentary understanding of key signatures, and have developed basic coordination skills on the recorder. During the first semester of beginning band, Herrings and his colleagues teach several exercises before any sound is made to reinforce proper hand position and the evenness of finger placement. Beginners are given a scale packet with various levels of achievement. At the top of the page is a five-note mini scale. The first level is a one-octave scale beginning on a half note and played in quarter notes. The second level is also one octave and starts on a quarter note with the scale played in eighth notes. The third level is a full range scale, with the goal being two octaves by the end of the first year, and there are usually some woodwind players that can successfully play the third octave.

Also included in the packet are supplemental exercises such as Cichowicz Flow Studies to develop smoothness in all ranges, Clarke Studies to reinforce articulation and technique, simple overtone slurs for the brass, and register slurs for the woodwinds. Herrings continuously monitors and comments on hand position while students count the line and tap their foot to a metronome or say the note names in tempo while moving their fingers accordingly. Overall, early study focuses heavily on fundamental exercises to build a solid foundation. Herrings said:

> I have learned over time that although we move slowly in sixth grade, there are concepts that can be taught quickly at the beginning of seventh grade when the students are more mature and have had more time on their instrument. This is why many of them can play grade-4 and grade-5 literature by the end of seventh grade.

Balance and Blend

When introducing the concept of balance and blend, Herrings draws attention to the location of each instrument at the first ensemble rehearsal. Beginning with the tubas and going in reverse score order, each section stands so students are aware of where they should be listening. Herrings then discusses the creation of new colors and timbres when instruments play together. He will often do "color drills" to explore different combinations of instruments and ask students where they should be listening. Herrings will also relate these subjective, complex concepts to something familiar like cooking, saying, "Each instrument is an important ingredient to the overall mix, and different tastes are the result of different combinations of those ingredients."

Herrings teaches students several rules for listening and finding an ideal ensemble balance: woodwinds color brass, clarinets should never play louder than flutes unless they are the melody, oboes should fit their sound inside the flutes, and flutes, oboes, and clarinets should fit their sound inside the trumpets.

Throughout the rehearsal process, Herrings frequently rewrites or rescores the music to achieve a clearer and more balanced ensemble sound. He said:

> Some composers do not understand instrument tendencies and range limitations with middle school students. For example, a tenor saxophone part might sound better if played with the third clarinets. Or, if the alto saxophones are in the more challenging low register, I will add the bassoons. Especially in slow music and older band repertoire, the textures are often very thick, and the melody is covered by accompanying lines or extended harmonies. Depending on the students, I will add instruments to the melody, so it is always the most prominent voice. Or, I will rewrite chords based on the ensemble's strengths and weaknesses to make the harmonies resonate. The changes are subtle but can make an enormous difference in the overall sound.

Words of Wisdom

When Herrings became director of bands at Henry, he had only three years of teaching experience. Luckily, great teachers were close by, and Herrings regularly observed their rehearsals and asked questions:

I would notice that their students had a different posture, hand position, and embouchure, and sounded much better. I would ask questions and fix my students the next day. I think the biggest mistake people make is that they do not ask questions or are afraid to ask questions. I have never been afraid to ask for help, and I will be the first person to tell my students that I do not know the answer. This approach is how I have built trust with them and why I think they respond to my criticism and expectation.

Herrings believes in measuring his success not by winning, but on retention of students. "If retention is less than 90 percent, that means the students do not feel successful or valued and my team and I are doing something wrong," he said. Over the years, Herrings has retained students and developed confident, mature musicians by setting the highest expectations, reinforced with love. He makes every attempt to connect with students outside of rehearsal by greeting them at the door every day, saying goodbye, and being observant and supportive of the student's life outside of band. He said:

I can push my students to a level they do not know they can accomplish because I have built a relationship with each of them that is based on trust and encouragement. It is about finding the balance between making them laugh, showing them you care about them as a student, and pushing them to be better. If they sometimes get mad at me in the process, that's okay. I tell them that if they are frustrated, I have done my job because it eventually translates into them doing something they did not know they could do and getting better as a result. They may not understand at the moment, but they do over time. It's expectation with love, and I think many directors feel they cannot push students and also make it fun. We have a lot of fun at Henry, but I teach my students that the work you put into something is what you get out of it. When it is all finished, I want my kids to say, "I am glad I did" instead of "I wish I had."

Cindy Lansford

"Teach like your hair is on fire."

Cindy Lansford retired in 2007 after thirty years of teaching middle and high school band. She earned a bachelor of music education degree from Texas Tech University and a master of education degree from Texas A&M University-Commerce.

Program Structure and Background

Cindy Lansford started her career as an assistant band director at her alma mater, Robert E. Lee High School, in Baytown, Texas. She later moved to Plano Senior High School in the Dallas suburbs before relocating to Baton Rouge, Louisiana. After leaving the profession for one year, Lansford returned to the Dallas-Fort Worth area, where she enjoyed a distinguished career as director of bands at Carpenter Middle School, assistant director of bands at Haltom High School, and director of bands at North Ridge Middle School. Lansford reflected on her growth as a teacher throughout her career:

> I always kept learning and growing wherever I taught. I think I learned how to be a great individual teacher when I was at Carpenter. While I was at Haltom, I learned so much from Eddie Green, and I think I learned how to teach an ensemble at North Ridge.

At Carpenter Middle School, 1,250–1,500 students were enrolled in grades six through eight, with 300–475 students in the band program.

102

Approximately 800 students attended North Ridge Middle School, with around 200–275 students enrolled in band. Both Carpenter and North Ridge had three concert bands in addition to homogenous beginner classes.

The concert bands met daily for fifty minutes, and the top ensemble always met during the lunch period because the administration never altered the length of that period, even during statewide testing. The three concert bands performed six concerts throughout the year: a fall, winter, and spring concert, plus a pre-contest, contest, and spring festival performance. During the first semester, students in the first and second bands prepared three etudes and scales as part of an all-region band audition. In January, every student participated in a chamber ensemble concert. Students in the top ensemble performed in traditional chamber groups. Students in the second band performed in sections, and students in the third band performed in choirs. For example, nine flutes in the second band played a standard flute trio, and the entire brass section of the third band performed a brass choir piece. In May, every student played a solo at a district-wide contest. Lansford described the curriculum approach:

> At the beginning of the year, we stressed individual improvement through music prepared for the all-region ensemble while mastering ensemble fundamentals in class. In late December and January, we stressed the chamber ensembles. Students could then apply those skills when we began our contest music in the second semester. We did solos at the end of the year when students were playing their best. It also kept them practicing at home until the end of the year.

Additional Instruction

Lansford taught sectionals year-round, before and after school, for each instrument in her ensemble. "In the full ensemble setting, students are not getting the individualized attention they need," she said. "For seventh and eighth graders, sectionals are advanced beginner band classes." In the first semester, Lansford taught fundamental concepts and prepared students for the all-region band auditions. In the second semester, sections were combined based on the needs of the concert music. "Sectionals allowed me to learn the strengths and weaknesses of each player, learn specifics about how to teach the instruments, and build relationships with my students," she said.

When Lansford first began teaching, private lessons were not encouraged or part of the school culture. However, as the expectation and standard in Texas grew, so did the desire for private lessons. Lansford explained:

> There are many myths about Texas that are not all true. We had many, but not all, students enrolled in private lessons with professionals in the area, and it was not required. It is expensive and a complicated process, depending on the school district. If students cannot afford lessons, I would hire high school or college students using fundraising dollars or assign recorded playing exams so they can get more specific information.

Ensemble Placement

At Carpenter, students auditioned for ensembles by playing scales and etudes in front of the entire section. "When I went to Haltom, I learned very quickly that this was not in the best interest of the student because students get even more nervous when they have to play individually in front of their peers," Lansford said. "It was not an adequate representation of their current playing ability." At North Ridge, students understood that auditions were a year-long process. Lansford related ensemble placement to math or science class; the top ensemble, honors band, was equivalent to a Pre-AP class and consisted primarily of eighth graders with a few seventh graders; the second band, symphonic band, was similar to an honors class with equal parts seventh and eighth graders; the third band, concert band, was the standard math class with mostly seventh graders and a few eighth graders. "If we did our job correctly, the seventh graders would progress to the honors band in eighth grade," she said.

Throughout the year, Lansford and her assistant would do individual pass-offs on the region or concert music. These were after school for ten minutes and allowed Lansford to learn more about the students, hear how they played, and assess their progress. Students would then play their major scales at the end of the year, which would either confirm or change Lansford's initial placement. Lansford never assigned chairs; instead, she rotated part assignments because "no kid ever wants to be labeled as last."

Instrumentation

Lansford continues to advocate for larger concert bands at the middle school level. "Smaller ensembles put undue and unnecessary pressure on students who are developing," she said. "More bodies will develop more confidence." The honors band never had less than sixty students: ten flutes, two or three oboes, two or three bassoons, ten to twelve clarinets, two bass clarinets, four alto saxophones, one tenor saxophone, one baritone saxophone, six French horns, ten trumpets, six trombones, three euphoniums, three tubas, and seven or eight percussionists.

In setting up her ensemble, Lansford preferred the flutes in the front row on the conductor's left, followed by oboes, bassoons, and first clarinets. "When the double reeds are proficient and can be placed in the front row, the ensemble will have a more mature, unique timbre," she said. The second row consisted of the second flutes, saxophone family, bass clarinets, and the remaining clarinets. The French horns sat to Lansford's left in the third row, followed by the trumpets on a low riser, and then euphoniums and tubas. The trombones sat behind the trumpets on a higher riser. Lansford explained:

> I liked having all the bell-front brass facing the audience. I have found over the years that the best sounding and most mature bands have equal parts trombone and trumpet. If the euphoniums can play well, I will move them into the second row because it adds a warmer color to the ensemble sound. I also put all of my best players on the ends, including the French horns.

The setup constantly fluctuated based on the selected music, solo requirements, desired timbre, section strength, and even the size and shape of the rehearsal space. "Do not be afraid to move kids," Lansford said. "Do what the music calls for or what the students need to sound good. In some cases, if the students are closer to a director, the sense of urgency raises."

Recruitment

Lansford operated under strict recruitment guidelines outlined by the administration. In some years, a music aptitude test was used to target fifth-grade students. In the second semester, all fifth graders visited the middle school, and each fine arts program gave a presentation. "I always promoted my kids and my program, saying that band kids were the best and smartest in the school," she said. "I talked about all of the activities they were involved in outside of band, like athletics and academics."

Lansford mailed out an informative brochure to each family, outlining the benefits of joining the band and answered frequently asked questions. She held a "band fair" during the second semester in which students and their parents chose three instruments to try, with the exception of percussion and saxophone. Lansford welcomed families at the door, and her assistant would advise parents and students at the end of the process. Local band directors would rate students, and Lansford's current students would assist at the instrument stations.

To make a good pairing of student to instruments, Lansford would assess the student's personality and physical characteristics. Flute players were typically the perfectionist, determined students. "You either can or cannot make a sound on flute," she said. She was also mindful of assigning boys to flute. "You have to know your community and the surrounding culture," she said. "I found that, in general, boys who are successful at playing flute have to have strong and independent personalities." Potential clarinet players had to have large enough finger pads to cover the tone holes. She would also see how they reacted to having the mouthpiece inside their mouth and touching their teeth. "Some students do not like the sensation and feel more comfortable having the mouthpiece on the outside of their lips," she said.

With double reeds, Lansford looked for smart, curious students who were comfortable standing out in a crowd. "You cannot be shy and play oboe or bassoon. These students need to be confident and not afraid of messing up because these are very difficult instruments that require a lot of trial and error." Lansford was also mindful of not placing overly athletic students on double reeds because the chances of them quitting later are higher, due to conflicting activity demands.

"Almost anyone can initially produce a sound on saxophone, as it is the most forgiving instrument with regard to facial structure," Lansford said. At the end of sixth grade, she would allow those interested in switching to tenor or bari to have a two-day trial period with each instrument. She and her assistant would then decide who was right for each instrument based on size, potential ability, and progress throughout the year on alto saxophone.

Lip size was the primary factor when placing brass students. "The most successful low brass players had full lips, and their corners were not very wide," Lansford said. She avoided putting students on high brass and flute if the middle part of a student's top lip hung down into their aperture, creating a tear-drop shape, which splits the air stream and makes it difficult to produce higher notes. Lansford tested the aural strength of prospective French horn players by singing and matching pitches and distinguishing the difference between high and low sounds.

Each year, Lansford attempted to recruit 40 percent of the fifth-grade class with no more than 150 beginners. "Anything more than that and you will lose them because they will not receive the individual attention or instruction needed to be successful," she said. Overall, Lansford believes visibility and maintaining a great relationship with the elementary music teachers and high school band directors was the key to successful recruitment.

Beginning Band Curriculum
At Carpenter and North Ridge, athletics were a separate class that met at the beginning and end of the school day. Since sixth graders were not involved, Lansford taught beginner classes during this time. Lansford always taught the beginning woodwind classes and occasionally the trumpet or trombone class. A percussion specialist was hired to teach the beginning percussion classes. Lansford stressed the importance of separating the woodwinds because it becomes hard for them to hear when they begin working in the upper registers. "To do this, my assistant and I used every possible room to make it work—the band hall, the stage, classrooms, orchestra and choir rooms, even the teacher's lounge."

Each of the three elementary feeder programs had strong music programs, but the students did not come to middle school reading music. This presented a challenge, but Lansford taught reading and instrument technique separately. "I taught sound before sight," she said. "We married the two at the end of the first six weeks when they could play simple songs out of the method book." Lansford never performed a fall concert with beginners because it forced students to quickly learn music, thus creating bad habits that were difficult to fix. The first beginning band concert occurred in the winter and was separate from the concert bands. Each section would perform a song, and the full ensemble would perform one easy piece together.

In her thirty years of teaching, every beginner class progressed differently in the first year, but the overall objectives remained the same. Her goal was for each student to play with a beautiful, characteristic tone quality, to articulate properly, and to be able to read notes and rhythms. Even when she taught beginner classes of mixed instruments, these priorities did not change; the only difference was the amount of material covered.

A key factor in Lansford's success with beginners was individual assessment on a daily basis. She said:

> It is tough to do, but I always moved between individual and group exercises. When I asked an individual to play a particular line, I would try to engage everybody in my feedback, because the rest of the students learned by listening to what I said. You have to find a creative, efficient system that allows you to get around the room quickly and hear everybody individually. Otherwise, students get lost in the mix and develop bad habits when you do not listen to them separately.

Overall, Lansford believes it is essential to be flexible when teaching beginners and always do what is required:

> Teaching beginning band is a long and slow process. In thirty years, I never got through the first method book because we went very slow at the beginning. By the first week of November, we were teaching eighth notes on page 11, but playing fun exercises from other books to reinforce fundamental concepts. If you have tenacity and persistence, students will cooperate.

Score Study and Rehearsal Preparation
Lansford always introduced difficult ensemble music in sectionals or small groups. She said:

> When I studied a score, I looked for the parts that we could play as a full ensemble and what parts I needed to save for sectionals. For example, when I taught Frank Ticheli's "Fortress", we spent a month on it in sectionals before playing it as a full ensemble. We would then work on the march or sections of another piece during class. When we finally played "Fortress" as an ensemble, the kids loved it, and that would not have been the case if we started at measure 1 on the first day.

Lansford spent each night assessing her rehearsals and making detailed lists of what to fix the following day. "The more mature the band, the more details and information I had to write down," she said. Lansford would also listen to recordings of her ensemble and then a recording of a professional ensemble, noting the differences in tone quality, timbre, balance, and clarity. She would then create a detailed plan for when and how to address those issues.

Tone

Producing a characteristic tone was Lansford's number-one priority for all beginners. Correct notes and rhythms, proper articulation and style, and musicality followed. "Students have to leave sixth grade with the same setup and same beautiful tone as a ninth or twelfth grader," she said. "The only difference is the fullness, range, refinement, and maturity of the sound."

Developing a proper embouchure was the first step, and since every student was different, experimentation was necessary. "Do not be afraid to experiment," she said. "Students are malleable at this age so if one approach is not working, find another, as it is much easier to fix at the beginning than later in the year." Lansford used mirrors to show students both correct and incorrect placement of the mouthpiece or head joint. "You have to keep putting it into their eyes and ears what is good and what is not acceptable."

Modeling was also essential at the beginning stages. Lansford would do call and response exercises on the mouthpiece or head joint, having students match her tone quality and articulation. She would then play a concert F on her instrument for four counts, rest for four counts, and students would play back. When students could perform this successfully, Lansford added various articulations. She also used students as models to help motivate others. "It's okay to create healthy competition in sectionals and push students to sound just as good as their friends," Lansford added.

By the end of the first year, the majority of woodwind players could play a two-octave chromatic scale, with some clarinets being able to play into the third octave. "Beginning clarinets are the most difficult to teach because there are so many students and there is so much more material to cover," she said. Bassoons would be able to play to F above the staff and oboes would go as high as C above the staff. With brass players, Lansford only taught what the students were physically able to do. However, students would still learn how to read and finger the notes they did not know. "Once you have set them up correctly," she said, "give them the right tools and resources and encourage them to figure out what they do not know on their own time."

Articulation and Style

Part of Lansford's daily fundamental routine included an exercise that began with a whole note, followed by two connected half notes, four connected quarter notes, four separated quarter notes, eight connected eighth notes, eight separated eighth notes, twelve triplets, and sixteen sixteenth notes. Lansford constantly addressed the quality of articulation and vertical alignment to refine the ensemble clarity. She said:

> Expose and fix! Go around the room in score order, reverse score order, or whatever combination of students to expose and fix those that are doing it differently. You have to define what exactly it is you want, how you are going to get what you want, and go after it until it is correct.

Many directors have students play these fundamental exercises without any music. However, Lansford's students always had their music open so they could read and interpret style markings. "You want students to react to the markings in their music when you are not there," Lansford said. "If they are not reading the music all the time, they are not reacting to it."

Technique

To develop technical coordination and dexterity, Lansford would start students with physical and mental exercises before having them make any sound. Students would say the note names out loud while tapping their foot to the metronome. They would then say the note names while putting down the correct fingers. When learning the chromatic scale, Lansford would often say the note name aloud while students found the right fingering, or she would have the students say and finger the note name while she played the note on her instrument. She explained:

> If students cannot play something, it is typically a note-recognition or a tempo issue. Many students will just put down the fingers but cannot say the note name. The physical and mental exercises set the students up to sound great on something the very first time. Then, when they played, I always tried to choose a tempo where they could be successful. If it was too fast, they did not sound good and bad habits formed. I have learned

that if kids do not like something, it is because they do not sound good and they know it.

To achieve a higher level of technical clarity, Lansford once again stressed the importance of exposing and fixing individual problems. "Going down the row terrifies kids," she said. "I would always have them play in groups, by rows, by grade, by what they were wearing—any random combination that still allows me to hear and assess individuals as I walk around the room."

Rhythm

"People have differing opinions on what is a characteristic tone, but with rhythm and technique, it is either right or wrong," Lansford said. In elementary school, most of her students had already learned to count rhythms on syllables like "ta" and "ti-ti", but it was not consistent across the student population. Therefore, she started over each year using the Eastman system because it reinforced proper articulation. "I have used and seen all the systems over the years, and they all have their pros and cons," Lansford said. "What matters is that you have a system and use it consistently."

Students learned to count rhythms and tap their toe to a metronome. "The physical sensation of tapping their toe and the coordination it requires helps build a steady internal pulse," Lansford said. "It was also a way for me to tell if a student can keep a steady pulse." She also used the metronome as a stabilizer for both her and the students. "It acts as a sort of checks and balances, so we all do not go too slow or too fast," she said. However, she was cautious of the volume of the metronome. "The metronome should be a guide and students should have to work to listen for it. It cannot be so loud that you cannot hear the starts and releases of notes or the ensemble sound."

Once students could count and finger an exercise or musical excerpt, they played the rhythm on a single pitch so that Lansford could address articulation, style, and vertical alignment. Then, students played the passage as written. "Many bands can count a passage with perfect alignment, but cannot play it nearly as well," she said. "We have to make sure we connect and transfer the skills from one to another."

Balance and Blend

In balancing her ensembles, Lansford favors color. "Woodwinds are the color and brass are the power," she said. "Color should not be louder than power." With younger players, this balance provides more fullness and depth to the overall ensemble sound.

She also encouraged students to listen across the band, continually reminding them of her guidelines for clear ensemble balance:

- When the full ensemble is playing, oboes must be able to hear the trumpets.
- If flutes and clarinets are in the same octave, clarinets must balance to the flute.
- If the clarinets are an octave lower than the flutes, flutes have to listen to the lower octave clarinets.
- If saxophones and clarinets are in unison, saxophones balance to clarinets.
- If the trumpets and woodwinds are playing, they should balance to the trumpets.
- Trombones and trumpets should be balanced equally.

Lansford taught students that most dynamic markings relate to the overall ensemble sound and not the individual player. Therefore, she would instruct students to rewrite dynamic markings for a more clear and textured balance. "Do not be afraid to rewrite dynamics or re-score parts to make your ensemble better," she said. "Highlight the strengths of your students to make your performance special and set it apart."

Words of Wisdom

Lansford encourages directors to attend conventions, teach summer band camps, and take advantage of any opportunities to learn from other directors and mentors:

When I first started, we did not have mentors, and nobody came to our rehearsals to help us. We just did the best we could. That has all changed now, and mentors are crucial. Find them, invite them to your rehearsals, and ask questions. There should always be more than one person listening to your ensemble throughout the year because everyone hears things differently and has different priorities for creating a great ensemble sound.

The best directors are the ones who keep learning and finding new ways to teach the same concept in many different ways.

Lansford believes that teaching middle school should set students up to be lifelong learners, and she recognizes that she is teaching much more than music:

> If you think something is important, they will too. If you think learning a scale is the coolest thing ever, the students will too. And if you can learn to correct a child without hurting their feelings, you can teach them anything. This ability takes time, and there is no secret. Everybody has to do it in their own personal way. Be confident in what you want, be articulate and thoughtful about how you want them to sound, and teach like your hair is on fire.

Everett McConn

"Band exists for the student; the student does not exist for the band."

Everett McConn has been the director of bands at Fort Clarke Middle School in Gainesville, Florida since 1998. He holds a bachelor's degree in music education from the University of Florida.

Career History

After graduating from the University of Florida, Everett McConn taught part-time at the P.K. Yonge Lab School in Gainesville, Florida. When he first arrived, only twenty-four students from grade six through twelve were enrolled in band. The program grew to sixty-five students after three years, and the ensemble made superior ratings at district marching and concert festivals. McConn then taught at Howard Bishop Middle School, where he discovered his passion for fundamentals. "That job showed me that my strength lies in my ability to teach the fundamentals of reading notes and rhythms, tone production, and shaping musical lines," he said. After his fourth year at Bishop, McConn left music education altogether and became the administrator of Living Faith Fellowship Christian School. He returned eleven years later and began working at a local music store to refresh and update his knowledge on instruments, mouthpieces, reeds, and repertoire. After one year, McConn returned to the classroom, spending two years at Price Middle School in Interlachen, Florida before moving to Fort Clarke Middle School in Gainesville in 1998. After having been an administrator, McConn reflected on his new perspective, saying:

When I returned to teaching, I had much more compassion for administrators. It is a big job involving many people who all think their program is the most important. They have limited resources and have to do what they feel is best for the whole picture, even if that may not be what is best for me.

Program Structure

Gainesville is a college town home to the University of Florida and Santa Fe College. Fort Clarke Middle School has approximately eight hundred students enrolled in grades six through eight and is the primary feeder of Buchholz High School. When McConn first arrived, Fort Clarke was on a seven-period day with 225–250 students in the band. Students could take two elective courses, which included band, chorus, drama, family and consumer sciences, art, technology, Spanish, or physical education. The concert bands were split by grade level, since electives for each grade occurred during the same period. The top ensemble, symphonic band, consisted of all eighth graders and the second and third bands were all seventh graders. McConn also had a seventh-grade beginning band and two sixth-grade beginning bands.

In 2002, the county moved to a six-period day to meet the demands of a statewide cap on class sizes. Students could only choose one elective, and as a result, the district eliminated chorus, art, and drama. As of 2018, there are 150–175 students in band, and McConn is the only band director. He teaches four concert ensembles that meet daily for fifty minutes. The symphonic band consists of the top woodwind and brass players and rehearses an additional two days a week before school. The concert band consists of seventh and eighth-grade woodwind and brass players who have at least one year of band class but are not ready or interested in the commitment required for symphonic band. The first beginning band class is for those who start at the beginning of the year while the second beginning band class is for those who began the summer prior. There is also an advanced percussion class comprised of all percussionists who have completed the beginning band class. Being separated allows these students to develop advanced skills on mallets, snare, and other concert percussion instruments. Select percussion students then rehearse with the symphonic band twice a week before school. Finally, jazz band meets before school twice a week for one hour and fifteen minutes.

Students understand that their ensemble audition is a year-long assessment of their progress and work ethic in class. However, on occasion, McConn will have students record and submit scales or conduct blind auditions. Students can also challenge their neighbor throughout the year for a higher chair placement. Each is given a week to prepare an etude or excerpt of the concert music and two or three scales, with sight-reading possibly included.

Selection for the symphonic band is based on skills, attitude, commitment, conduct, what is best for the individual student, and what is best for the balance of the program. The ensemble typically has four to eight flutes, two oboes, two to three bassoons, twelve clarinets, two or three bass clarinets, an E-flat contra-alto clarinet if possible, three alto saxophones, two tenor saxophones, one or two baritone saxophones, seven trumpets, six French horns, six trombones, four euphoniums, five tubas, and seven percussionists. However, these numbers have fluctuated over the years.

The symphonic band performs a fall, winter, and spring concert as well as at Music Performance Assessment (MPA), a statewide assessment organized by the Florida Bandmasters Association. They also perform at four elementary schools, various school assemblies, the local Veterans Day celebration, and in-school caroling before winter break. The concert band plays at the winter and spring concerts and MPA. All symphonic and concert band students are required to participate in the Florida Bandmasters Association solo and ensemble MPA. If a beginning band student is taking private lessons, they can participate as well. McConn holds an event at Fort Clarke prior to the solo and ensemble festival, and local band directors offer feedback to the students without a rating.

Students can also audition for the Florida all-state band and the Alachua County honor band. McConn praised the value of these audition-based ensembles:

> Any performance opportunity outside of class is the best thing we can do for our programs to develop individual, independent players. Kids hate it the first time and are scared to death. But afterward, they are excited and motivated to practice, so it is worth every bit of extra time involved to make it happen.

Double-reed players are the only students required to take private lessons. Enrollment for other instruments is challenging, with many middle/lower-income families and 45 percent of the students on free-and-reduced lunch. The school district provides a small amount of funding per year, but McConn has an active band booster organization that offers substantial monetary support. The boosters hold two breakfast fundraisers and three significant fundraisers each year, the most successful of which is an onion sale, which brings in thousands of dollars. Profits from the fundraisers allow the boosters to pay for sectional coaches, instrument repairs, music purchases, and entry fees and accompanists for all solo and ensemble participants. The student's fair-share account receives profits from the remaining fundraisers. The fair-share program is an annual contribution ($145 for symphonic band, $100 for concert band, and $80 for beginning band) that can be paid directly or fundraised. While it is voluntary, students must have contributed to travel and participate in band activities outside of class. "Families that cannot afford the fair-share fee may fill out an annual request for financial assistance," McConn said. "No student is ever kept from participating because of money."

Recruitment

McConn recruits students from four elementary schools. The symphonic band plays at each elementary school during the first semester. Additionally, McConn visits the sixth-grade lunches to promote the seventh-grade beginning band. Students can then sign up to participate in summer band, a two-week program combined with another middle school. Students meet from 8:30 a.m.–12:30 p.m., Monday through Friday, with jazz band meeting from 1:00–2:30 p.m. Summer band is open to any middle school student, and typically 30 to 35 percent of the participants are beginners.

Two days before summer band, students select their instruments. If they choose to not participate in summer band, they select their instruments after school during the first week of classes. McConn bases instrument selection on three factors:

> The first is the student's natural ability to produce a good sound and for brass players to hit various partials. They must have the ability to make a proper embouchure, get a good sound on the mouthpiece or head joint, or play the correct pitches on the saxophone mouthpiece or clarinet barrel. You must also notice physical characteristics, such as their teeth, finger

size, and arm length. The second factor is the student's desire. It has been my experience that when I forced a student to play an instrument they did not want to play, I usually lost them. If their heart is set on something, we typically allow them to try it. The third factor is the needs of the program. I try to guide particular instruments based on the ensemble needs. However, my experience has been that balance issues usually work themselves out.

If it is obvious a student is on the wrong instrument, McConn makes every effort to switch them as soon as possible. He usually gives several individual lessons to get them started and then has an advanced beginner or eighth grader assist the student. McConn has found particular success in switching trumpet players who could not play above the staff to euphonium or tuba. In fact, over the years, McConn seeks out low brass players first. "If I can find students to play those instruments first, the other instruments will fall easily in place," he said.

Beginning Band Curriculum
McConn believes in setting a high expectation from the beginning and continuously reminding students that learning an instrument is a slow process. Each year, he typically has sixty to eighty beginners divided into two heterogeneous classes. The first class is made up of students who attended summer band, and the other is for sixth and seventh graders who begin in the first semester. Regardless of the class, the goals for the first three weeks are identical. McConn expects students to have proper posture, hand position, and embouchure placement. The basics of reading music are addressed using workbooks like *Excellence in Theory* and *Fundamentals of Music Theory for the Wind Band Student.* McConn uses *Winning Rhythms* to define pulse, demonstrate meter, teach students how to tap their toe, and count simple rhythms on the "1-e-and-uh" system. McConn also stresses the three points of posture ("feet flat on the floor, rump on the hump, back arched") and the three points of breathing ("we breathe through the mouth, from the diaphragm, and in time"). Finally, students learn to sing simple melodies on solfege.

By the end of the first year, he expects that students understand how to breathe, are able to play various dynamic levels and tempos, and are able to count and perform rhythms using whole, half, quarter, eighth, and sixteenth notes and their corresponding rests. He also wants students to be able to play the concert G, C, F, B-flat, E-flat, and A-flat scales and their major arpeggios, as well as a two-octave chromatic scale with a characteristic tone quality in all ranges.

With middle school students, McConn also stressed the importance of setting up the room, so there is access to every student. He explained:

> One of the easiest and biggest pitfalls in teaching band is to get stuck on the podium. I put an aisle down the middle of the band and have plenty of room between rows so there is access to every student, and I can fix hand position, posture, and embouchure while hearing them in the context of the full group.

Finally, McConn learned from his colleague, Jim Matthews, that it is vital to hear students play every single day. He said:

> It is tough and not always achievable, but it is still my goal. I pick something short and reasonable, maybe one note or a scale passage, and others are silent, which teaches them patience and rehearsal focus. Or I find ways to include them, like singing, fingering along, or having brass players buzz while others sing.

Score Study and Rehearsal Preparation

As the sole director of the program, McConn works approximately eleven hours a day and balances this with being present for his family, including six grandchildren. Not surprisingly, he struggles to find time for serious score study. "Middle school music does not require much depth of study, but detailed planning with the students in mind is necessary at this level," he said. McConn typically sings through each line of the score, being aware of potential issues in range, technique, rhythm, and balance or blend. If possible, he will also play through each part on the written instrument. "This helps identify fingering issues and determine where to use chromatic or alternate fingerings, where to breathe, and whether the dynamic markings are appropriate." McConn then sight-reads through the piece with the students, listening carefully and analyzing the difficulties ahead. He addresses those issues in the context of the warmup by adapting his fundamental daily routine. "You always have to be responding to what the students are doing," McConn said. "Every day is different, and each rehearsal highlights new problems that need to be addressed the following day."

Repertoire Selection

When choosing music, McConn searches for a variety of contrasting works that are conceptually based. Although he repeats a few standards, McConn tends to perform newer music that appeals to middle school students and teaches the same conceptual ideas. He always performs a march, a lyrical piece, and challenging composition he knows the students will enjoy working on for an extended period. "A march reinforces technical skills, articulation concepts, and introduces concepts of style and balance," he said. "I also believe students have to play something beautiful that has intriguing melodies and a variety of colors."

When finished with the district assessment, McConn continues challenging the students for the spring concert. He said:

> I always see directors perform easy, fun music at the end of the year. However, I want students to continue growing so we do a technically difficult work that is still fun. It's all in the way you sell it to your students. Regardless of the music you pick, we have to fight the urge to get through the method book or get ready for the concert. We have to use the music instead to teach the child how to play the instrument. When you do that, everything is achievable.

Tone

McConn reinforces his three points of posture and three points of breathing using hand motions: "Feet flat on the floor, rump on the hump, back arched. We breathe through the mouth, from the diaphragm, and in time." He then begins with breathing exercises, so students understand the amount of air needed to play their instrument. "Air is magic and will typically fix 95 percent of whatever is wrong," he said. He referenced his teacher, Frank Wickes, who once said:

> Until students can play loudly with a full tone, they cannot play at a soft dynamic level. They may be able to get a sound, but they cannot control the soft dynamic until they understand how to breathe correctly and use their air to play *forte* with a characteristic tone and accurate intonation.

McConn always begins rehearsal with long tones, lip slurs for the brass, and register slurs for the woodwinds. He models a proper tone quality and has students sustain a note for four, eight, twelve, or sixteen counts. "Many people only hold long tones for four or maybe eight counts," he said. "We forget we have to teach students how to sustain for sixteen counts without changing the tone quality or intonation."

Intonation

"We teach tuning by teaching them to be conscious of listening," McConn said. Students learn about intonation once posture, embouchure, and hand position are consistent, air is moving correctly through the instrument, and they can make accurate and characteristic sounds on the mouthpiece, barrel, or head joint. Then, McConn begins teaching students how and why they need to adjust the instrument length and the importance of matching their neighbor. He starts with two students playing one pitch and uses the Tonal Energy app or digital tuner to guide students' ears on what is correct and not correct. Then, McConn teaches students how to overcome the inherent flaws of the instrument:

> Clarinets have to learn that when they are crossing the break, they put the right hand down on G, A-flat, A, and B-flat, so all they have to worry about is the left-hand register key. Trumpet players have to experiment with alternate fingerings on fourth-line D and fourth-space E and learn how and why to lip them up.

To continue developing aural awareness and pitch internalization, students sing concert B-flat, F, and C each day with and without a reference. Students also sing scales and various scale patterns on solfege with the corresponding hand signs. McConn often splits the ensemble in half, and one half will sing the first half of the scale and the other half finishes it. Or, McConn will play the first note of the scale and students have to sing whatever hand sign he gives. When students can successfully do this, McConn moves to basic chord progressions. He said:

> When I teach intonation, I am teaching students about pitch and interval relationships. We play, then sing, then play, continuing to refine and adjust. Students will sing on a neutral syllable like "dah" or "di," and the brass will buzz through it to help pitch accuracy. When I was a young teacher, I was so dependent on the machine rather than developing their ear. Now, I want them to be consciously listening at all times and develop the skills so they can adjust in the moment.

Rhythm

When teaching rhythm to beginners, McConn believes in the "say, tap, clap" system, in which students tap their foot to the metronome while clapping and saying the rhythms. "We are essentially trying to teach multitasking, because they will often try to tap the rhythm instead of tapping the beat," he said. McConn also insists that percussionists count aloud while playing, to build coordination. "If their hands will do what their mouth does, they will be correct 90 to 95 percent of the time." When students count out loud, McConn stresses the importance of counting rests as "silent notes." "We have to teach younger students that a rest does not mean to rest," he said. "I learned from Shawn Barat at Buchholz High School to refer to them as 'silent notes' to show they are just as important as notes they play."

McConn teaches several rules regarding rhythm. The first is that when a long note connects to a short note, the short note is the release point. He will tell students, "Hold to it, not through it" or "Hold the notes and don't relax the lips until the sound stops." Additionally, notes shorter than a quarter note are separated and quarter notes or longer should be played full value unless the style of music dictates otherwise. Regarding syncopation, he said:

> When there is a 4 in the bottom of the time signature and a quarter note starts on the beat, whatever comes after it will start on the next beat. If a quarter note begins on the "and" of the beat, whatever comes after it will start on the next "and." This seems obvious, but syncopation can be a difficult concept for middle school students to understand.

Technique

When teaching beginners to build technical dexterity and coordination, McConn stressed the importance of teaching correct hand position and articulation first. "Students have to keep their fingers close to the keys and understand how the tongue and fingers align before they can build skill," he said. When teaching any passage where accuracy is a problem, McConn isolates the passage, playing one note at a time until everyone has the correct key signature, fingering, articulation, and pitch in their ear. Then, he plays it slowly, in rhythm, focusing on accuracy of each musical element. The passage is repeated slowly and accurately numerous times to build muscle memory. He will also alter or reverse the rhythm, so students play groups of two, one note long plus three short notes, or three short notes plus one long note. Then, once the trouble spot improves, McConn begins the measure before the trouble spot and plays until the measure after to connect the musical line. "Practice makes permanent, perfect practice makes perfect," he said. "Therefore, I go as slow as needed for it to be right and for everybody to feel successful."

Balance and Blend

McConn uses Francis McBeth's "pyramid of sound" concept to teach students about ensemble balance and where to direct their listening. "When the full ensemble plays, bass voices play the strongest, followed by baritone, tenor, alto, and soprano voice, to create the warmest and richest depth of sound," he said. He uses chorales to experiment with playing in and out of balance and changing the dynamic of different instrument groups. Students compare and contrast the resulting timbre and gradually develop a definition of ideal balance. McConn also uses similar exercises to teach students about melodic priority. Instruments with the counter-melody and harmonic accompaniment play stronger than those with the melody. Through guided questioning, students discover why the melody needs to be the dominant voice. "The goal is to strike a balance between melodic priority and ensemble timbre, depending on what is called for in the music," he said.

McConn describes the concept of ensemble blend using the homogenization process of milk. He said:

> When I talk about ensemble blend, I use the idea of milk as it comes straight from the cow. When milk sits, a bit of the cream will rise to the top, leaving a waterier substance below. When we put it through the homogenization process, it stays together so the different parts of the milk cannot be readily distinguished. In the band, we want a sound in which the different voices blend so that no single sound sticks out above the others.

Words of Wisdom

To develop a culture of excellence within the band program, McConn believes teachers must define what excellence is, demonstrate it, and demand it of the students. He does an awards program at the end of the year to recognize outstanding woodwind, brass and percussion players from each band. He also gives a Director's Award to the student who represents the commitment and responsibility of an ideal band student. McConn also distributes P.R.I.D.E awards to each student who shows a Positive attitude, Respect, Individual responsibility, Discipline, and Excellence throughout the year. "Our culture of excellence began when the beginners saw and were inspired by watching their friends earn these awards," he said.

Finally, McConn believes his job as a music educator is to teach students to master the skills necessary to make music without him, outside of the band room. Most importantly, he believes the band exists for the student; the student does not exist for the band. He said:

> A student's value as a person is not dependent on what they can contribute to the success of the band. Students, as people, are not what they are ultimately going to be. Therefore, I teach my students kindness and truth, and that successful people do the things unsuccessful people will not do. What we do should be as much about life as about music because most students will not grow up to be professional musicians. However, learning how to treat people, resolve conflicts, manage their time, and work as a team, as well as experience the reward of hard work under inspired leadership, will go with them forever.

Heath and Christine Wolf

"If we are not happy with what is happening in our band, we start with ourselves."

Heath Wolf is currently the director of bands at Farmington Junior High School in Farmington, Utah. He earned a bachelor of music education and master of music degree from the University of Utah. Christine Wolf is currently the director of bands at Central Davis Junior High School in Layton, Utah. She earned a bachelor of music education degree from the University of Utah.

Program Structure

After graduating from the University of Utah, Heath Wolf was hired as a music specialist by the Catholic diocese to teach band and general music to more than 800 students at four different elementary and junior high schools. He moved to Hillcrest Junior High School in the center of the Salt Lake Valley after two years, where he taught band, orchestra, and general music. Five years later, Heath became director of bands at Farmington Junior High School in Farmington, Utah. Farmington Junior High School is located north of Salt Lake City and has an enrollment of approximately 1,150 students in grades seven through nine, with more than 400 students participating in band.

Christine Wolf began her teaching career as the director of bands at American Fork Junior High School in American Fork, Utah. When their first child was born, Christine began teaching privately, remained an active woodwind clinician, and assisted Heath as the band program at Farmington continued to grow. In 2010, she was hired part-time at Farmington as an assistant band director. However, no junior high school in the surrounding area employs a full-time assistant director, so to earn retirement credit, Christine was also hired part-time at Central Davis Junior High School in Layton, Utah. There were forty-five students in the band program when she arrived, and after three years, the program grew to where she was needed full-time. There are about 1,000 students currently enrolled in grades seven through nine at Central Davis, with more than 250 students participating in band.

Each day, Heath teaches two concert bands, jazz band, advanced percussion, beginning flute and double reeds, beginning clarinet and saxophone, beginning brass, and beginning percussion. On Monday and Wednesday, each class is fifty minutes long. On Tuesday and Thursday, classes are forty-five minutes due to an advisory period, and on Friday, classes are forty minutes due to mandatory staff development.

At Central Davis, Christine teaches on a rotating block schedule with seventy-minute classes every day except Fridays. Like Heath, classes are sixty minutes on Friday to allow for staff development. On "A" days, Christine teaches beginning percussion, beginning woodwinds, beginning brass, and jazz band. She teaches two concert bands, advanced percussion, and a general music class on "B" days.

The bands at both Farmington and Central Davis perform four concerts per year. The top ensemble at each school, symphonic band, has additional satellite performances at the elementary schools, local and national festivals, and the Utah state band festival. The jazz bands will regularly perform around the community, and both percussion ensembles participate in the Percussive Arts Society's "Day of Percussion" competition every year. Students at both schools can participate in a district solo and ensemble competition. Only a limited number of students from each school can attend, so they must qualify by receiving a superior rating at a schoolwide competition. Students can also audition for an all-district band and newly formed all-state middle school band. For the Wolfs, negotiating so many performance opportunities can be a challenge. Heath said:

Our students are involved in so many sports and extracurricular activities besides band that we try to find balance in the number of performances we have each year. We cannot forget that they are students who also need to fulfill their academic requirements.

Ensemble Placement

When placing students in ensembles, Heath described the challenges given his current situation:

I have learned that ninth graders will quit if they have to repeat the concert band class because the majority of the class are eighth-grade students. Unfortunately, there is no room in my schedule for another concert band, but I believe it is my responsibility to send as many students as possible to the high school program. So, I put them in symphonic band, which is why this ensemble has more students than the average.

The top ensemble at Farmington typically has nine flutes, two oboes, ten clarinets, three or four bass clarinets, two bassoons, eight trumpets, six horns, eight trombones, two euphoniums, and four tubas.

Students at Central Davis understand that auditions are a year-long assessment. Most eighth graders will play in concert band and move to symphonic band in ninth grade, except for a few students who are encouraged to remain in concert band. Once Christine places all rising ninth graders, rising eighth-grade students can then audition for any available spots in the top ensemble.

Additional Instruction

Only a small portion of students take private lessons, but students in the top ensemble organize sectionals before school, once a week. At the beginning of the year, Heath and Christine teach students how to run an efficient sectional. Section leaders are given specific tasks to accomplish and must submit a form summarizing the tasks completed and the effectiveness of the sectional. Christine said:

With four kids between two full-time band directors, we do not have the time to teach sectionals during the week. However, we teach our students how to run a sectional, what to listen for, and how to fix it. We hold them accountable, and by monitoring their progress, they are always able to meet the expectation.

Funding

The state of Utah has one of the lowest per-pupil expenditures in the country, and statewide arts funding is low. Both Heath and Christine receive minimal funds from the administration to purchase music, which is put in the same category as textbooks, and equipment. To help meet budget needs, Heath holds two fundraisers at Farmington each year. The first is a Halloween concert in conjunction with the orchestra and choir. For the second fundraiser, students raise thousands of dollars selling ice cream sandwiches. At Central Davis, Christine has a similar fundraising concert during the holiday season. She has also received substantial support through government school land grants, which has allowed her to rebuild her inventory over the past six years.

Recruitment

Heath recruits sixth-grade students from five elementary schools, and Christine has seven partial feeder programs. Both have similar recruitment processes. In December, the jazz band and symphonic band perform at every elementary school. These assemblies are for the entire elementary school, grades kindergarten through six, so students experience the band from an early age. The symphonic band and jazz band play standard holiday music, such as "Jingle Bells" and "Frosty the Snow Man," and the elementary students sing along. Section leaders demonstrate their instrument and play recognizable pop tunes or movie melodies. Sixth graders are invited to sit with the band on the last piece. "The elementary principals love it," said Christine. "It is their favorite assembly of the year because of the energy and excitement of the band students."

A week before course registration, Heath and Christine have an "instrument petting zoo" at the elementary schools. Heath and Christine demonstrate the instruments, and students can try them. They also distribute detailed information about how to sign up for beginning band. At Central Davis, instrument selection occurs on the same night as students register for classes. "I do this because, at my school, we might get the parents to school once, but we will not get them there twice," Christine said. Students sample the instruments once again, and Christine does not create a predetermined instrumentation. She typically allows students to choose the instrument they will enjoy playing the most, pending no physical issues

At Farmington, Heath is much more particular about beginning band instrumentation. Interested students register, and once Heath has a total number, he plans a maximum number of each instrument. He said:

> To have a balanced instrumentation, directors must guide students towards the instruments needed. We do not force students, but beginners do not know if they love it or not, so it is our job to sell it to them. If you do not control it, the product will not be as successful and the risk of students quitting is higher because it is not a great experience.

When placing students on instruments, Heath learns more about the student's personality. He asks questions to determine whether they have previously studied an instrument, their ability to sing on pitch, their grades in school, and whether they are a high-functioning and organized student. "Especially with French horn and double reed players, having strong aural skills and a determined personality are essential," he said. Brass players will buzz on different mouthpieces, and Heath will use a Pneumo Pro Wind Director with potential flute players to see if they can direct their air in a specific way. Neither Heath and Christine start students on saxophone, tuba, or euphonium until halfway through seventh grade. They choose saxophone players from the clarinet class, and euphonium and tuba players from the trombone class. Heath said:

> We typically have eighty beginning brass players so the less variety, the better. Also, switching from slide to valves is much easier than trying to switch a student who is struggling with euphonium or tuba back to trombone. If students can successfully use their air to play trombone, switching to euphonium or tuba should be pretty easy.

Once students sign up for beginning band, Heath and Christine provide a recommended list of equipment with preferred music stores listed first. Since some of their students cannot afford high-quality equipment such as mouthpiece barrels or ligatures, they will often buy classroom sets. Christine encourages directors to build relationships with instrument representatives at state and national conventions. As a clarinet player, representatives from Backun and Yamaha allowed her to sample their new beginning clarinet. Her students played on it and found it significantly more comfortable to cross the break. "Once the students experienced the difference for themselves, they were more motivated to go to the music store and rent that instrument," she said.

Beginning Band Curriculum

The summer before seventh grade, beginning band students at both Farmington and Central Davis meet for three weeks in homogeneous classes. Central Davis students meet in June, and Farmington students meet in August. Heath teaches the brass and percussion classes while Christine teaches the woodwind classes. Students learn how to assemble the instrument correctly, form a correct embouchure, and play with correct posture and hand position. "With mixed classes during the school year, this allows students to be functional on the first day," Heath said. At the beginning of the year, students who attended summer band are seated next to those who did not. Additionally, Heath and Christine have several teaching assistants who help with the beginning band classes. These are typically advanced ninth-grade band students, and they assist individuals and small sections or help proctor *SmartMusic* assessments.

Both Heath and Christine use the *Essential Elements* series because they find the curriculum to be more beneficial for heterogeneous classes. The beginning classes typically complete the first book and half of the second in the first year. However, both Heath and Christine are primarily concerned with how students play and not how much material they cover. Heath said:

> When I first started, I made the mistake of having a set plan of where the students should be by a specific date. This schedule forces some students to move faster than they can, and, in the process, develop bad habits that are difficult to undo. We have to teach students where they are at and tell beginners that they will progress differently. In the end, students advance quicker when there is no pressure to move at a specific pace and the process is not forced.

Beginners at Farmington have weekly playing tests, usually on Friday, so that Heath can assess individual progress. Since Central Davis is on a block schedule, Christine loses six weeks of instruction over the course of the year compared to Heath. Therefore, she has to reduce the time devoted to assessments. "I have revamped this system every year because every class has required a different approach," she said. For each playing exam,

Heath and Christine turn on the metronome, and each student plays the assigned fundamental exercise, scale, or melody. The Wolfs have created a rubric that allows them to provide feedback to each student quickly. If a student is dissatisfied with their grade, they can retake the playing exam as many times as possible. When students are not playing, they are silently working on music theory using the *Five-Minute Theory* workbook or practicing silently.

Both Christine and Heath incorporate many activities into the beginning band classes to supplement the method book. For example, they have a rubber ball with various musical terms drawn on it. Students throw the ball to one another, and wherever their right thumb lands, they have to define that term. The Wolfs also have a karate-inspired incentive system. Three playing assignments correspond to karate belt colors and the requirements for each color progress in difficulty. If the student receives an 80 percent or higher on each playing test, they receive a colored ring to put on their instrument case. The students that have earned a black belt by the end of the year get a pizza party.

"Sometimes I feel like my beginner classes are like Sea World; do something good and get a fish. However, instead of fish, we give candy," joked Heath. During class, Heath and Christine will choose individuals to play using an empty box of cereal and poker chips. The students are assigned a number that is written on a poker chip and placed in an empty box of cereal. Heath or Christine will draw a poker chip, and the student with the corresponding number chooses to play or not. If the student plays it correctly, they get a piece of candy. If they do not, the piece of candy goes into a bowl, and the next student can earn two pieces of candy if they play it right.

On Fridays, after playing assessments, the Wolfs will also have a competition in the style of *The Hunger Games*. Everybody stands up, the metronome is turned on, and the students start playing from the beginning of the method book. If a student makes a mistake, they must sit down and continue fingering along. The last student standing and the last section standing wins a prize. "The teacher dictates the atmosphere of the rehearsal," Christine said. "We always try to be creative, make it fun, and minimize the pressure. If the teacher is excited about it, the students will be too."

Both Heath and Christine believe the key to successfully teaching beginners is knowing the specific pedagogy of the instruments. Heath said:

> I learned from renowned conductor Anthony Maiello to analyze, diagnose, and prescribe. Many beginning band directors lack the skills and knowledge to prescribe the solution. They can hear who and what is wrong, but not how to fix it. This ability takes time, but it requires learning the specifics of the instruments. And, if I do not know how to fix an issue, I move on and always make sure I have the answer by the next rehearsal.

Repertoire Selection

Both Heath and Christine agree that they have to be excited about the music so that their students will be excited as well. They avoid choosing music designed to teach concepts; instead, they teach those concepts in the fundamental warmup and apply them to the piece. Heath explained:

> I do not choose a piece because it is in a compound meter. If a piece that I know my kids will enjoy playing every day happens to be in a compound meter, we will teach that concept through fundamental exercises first and transfer those skills to the piece.

At each concert, the jazz band, beginning band, concert band, and symphonic band perform, so Heath and Christine need to be mindful of the overall program length. They typically program three to five compositions per ensemble, per concert, and choose music based on the progress of each section and the overall ensemble. Christine said:

> We have a group of pieces we will consider playing, but it is difficult to predict how a middle school band will develop throughout the first semester. We teach them where they are at and choose music that fits the strengths and weaknesses of the ensemble.

Score Study and Rehearsal Preparation

The couple agree that it is a challenge to prepare adequately with busy home lives, but they have still found ways to achieve their student goals. "When you teach all day without a planning period and have four children at home, it is nearly impossible to do proper score study and rehearsal planning," Christine said. However, she makes time to create a structured plan, since she rehearses two or three times a week on the block schedule. "When I have a concert, I will map out how much time we spend on each piece at each rehearsal," she said. "I have to hold myself accountable, so we do not get behind in our preparation."

Heath feels that working on fundamentals makes things easier in full-band rehearsal. "If you are teaching musical concepts and reinforcing fundamentals on a daily basis," he said, "the process of learning music should be fairly quick."

Both Heath and Christine listen to and compare recordings of professional ensembles to their ensemble rehearsals. They take detailed notes on what needs to be fixed and distribute those lists to the students. Heath and Christine also inform section leaders of what items to address in sectionals and how to fix them.

Tone

Both Christine and Heath believe that providing an aural model and daily rehearsal of fundamental exercises are essential for developing individual and ensemble tone quality. They frequently model on their instrument and use the teaching assistants to demonstrate in the beginner classes. Additionally, the Wolfs bring in local professionals about once a month to play, model, and assist with instrument-specific instruction. Throughout the year, Heath and Christine will have students compare and contrast a professional recording or a recording of another middle school band with their own. "We talk about why they do not sound like that," Heath said. "I always tell them that if other middle school students can do it, so can they."

Students are expected to be in their seats sixty seconds after the tardy bell rings, doing breathing exercises through PVC pipes with an adjustable valve. "Everybody is silent except for the sound of air moving," Christine said. "A calm settles over the ensemble and breathing helps focus the rehearsal." When students play long-tone exercises, Heath and Christine use the visualizer on the Tonal Energy App to show them the shape of their sound. "Beginning students typically have harsh, violent, and inconsistent sounds," Heath said. "The goal is for students to move their air calmly, smoothly, and be a consistent block of sound."

After completing the second *Essential Elements* method book, the second concert band uses *Habits of a Successful Middle School Musician*, published by GIA. The top ensemble uses *Foundations for Superior*

Performance, published by Kjos. These method books increase the student's range using Remington long-tone exercises, lip slurs, and register slurs. Woodwind players will play the exercise, sing the exercise, and play the exercise again to internalize pitch and emulate the voice in their tone quality. Brass players frequently buzz but will hold the mouthpiece between their third and fourth fingers on their left hand, with the hand facing backward and parallel to the lips. Heath said:

> We put the mouthpiece in their weak hand between their weak fingers, so they do not have the strength to press the mouthpiece into the face; it just rests on their mouth. We call it "spocking" since their left hand forms Spock's famous hand sign from *Star Trek.*

Heath and Christine also use BERPS, a tool that attaches to the instrument and adds resistance to the buzz. Students will also sizzle as they exhale their air to learn how to sustain and distribute their air evenly over time. "To develop a wide range on the instrument, students have to learn how to use their air efficiently and in specific ways, depending on their instrument," Christine said.

Intonation

Students at Farmington and Central Davis are expected to sing every day from the first day of beginning band. Heath encourages students to use their husky "football player" or "opera singer" voice and to be confident, even if it is wrong at first. "We do not judge them or make them sing in public," Heath said. "Younger students see the symphonic band singing every day, so they do not question why we do it. It is just what we do."

Students sing fundamental exercises on a neutral syllable or the note names before playing them. They sing chorales or excerpts of the music to develop their inner ear and aural awareness. They both agreed, "The goal is always to match their instrument to their voice and hear the music in their head before transferring it to the instrument."

At the end of the year, once the final concert is over, one of Heath's favorite activities is for students to pick a favorite song and perform the verse and chorus in front of the class. "After spending so much time during the year focusing on reading, we focus on the ears," he said. "The students are not allowed to find the music or use it when they perform. It's a great way to assess their aural abilities."

Rhythm

"As a young teacher, I thought most errors I heard were technical when they were, in fact, rhythmic," Heath said. "Many directors assume their students understand rhythm, pulse, and subdivision, but we have to be careful because many learn by rote." Heath and Christine use the rhythmic exercises in the appendix of *Essential Elements* and the method book *101 Rhythmic Rest Patterns* to teach rhythmic reading. The beginner classes have a competition to see which class can perform the exercises without any mistakes. "We are very strict about rhythm and will not go on until the entire ensemble plays it correctly," Heath said. Students count, clap, and sizzle the exercise with a metronome. "You have to use a metronome when you teach beginners, or they are not going to learn a sense of consistent pulse," Christine said. The Wolfs will put the metronome on quarter notes for the first time through, then play the exercise again with the metronome on half notes, and then play it once more with the metronome on the whole note. They also will start the metronome, turn down the volume as students are playing, and then turn the volume back up to check the consistency of the tempo.

When Heath and Christine encounter a rhythmically complex passage, they use an exercise called "bopping" to reinforce subdivision and fix vertical alignment. Students play every note as if it were an eighth note, which creates a "bop" sound. By eliminating the sustained rhythmic value, the ensemble can focus on articulating the rhythm the same way, at the same time. Students bop the rhythm first on a concert F, and once the vertical alignment is correct, they will add the notes. "Any time there is a difficult passage, we break it down to its simplest element and sequentially build their skills," Heath said. "We count the rhythm, count the rhythm while fingering or positioning, bop the rhythm on a concert F, bop the rhythm on the written notes, and then play the passage as written."

Technique

When developing technique, seventh-grade beginners learn five-note scales and eighth and ninth graders play one-octave scales. Heath and Christine use a book called *Pathways to Power* to teach beginners about accidentals, enharmonic equivalents, and chromatic notes. Exercises are typically eight measures long and only use quarter notes and half notes in a range appropriate for beginners. The exercises are designed to develop chromatic awareness and facility, as opposed to reinforcing the patterns of a given key signature. As a result, beginners understand there is no difference between G-flat and F-sharp or C-flat and B-natural.

With eighth and ninth graders, Heath and Christine use an unpublished book called *Chatlands* to develop technical coordination. The book includes four exercises in all twelve keys: a scale played in stepwise motion in the first exercise, in thirds in the second exercise, as an arpeggio in the third exercise, and with various articulations in the fourth exercise. The Wolfs also use "toggle" and "ladder" patterns when practicing scales. "Toggle" patterns alternate notes of the scale in stepwise motion: "C–D–C–D" followed by "D–E–D–E" and so forth on a C-major scale. "Ladder" patterns add one note of the scale in each sequence: "C–D–C" followed by "C–D–E–D–C" and so forth on a C-major scale.

Students must play their scales from memory as part of their final exam. To prepare, Heath and Christine play "band basketball." Students are lined up in a row, and each student plays one of the twelve scales with a metronome. If the student plays it wrong, the entire class plays the scale. If the student plays it correctly, they shoot a basketball. If they make the first shot, the student can choose the tempo for their final playing exam. If they make a second shot, they are exempt from the test. The section can choose the tempo for the final exam if the student makes the third shot. Finally, if the student makes four consecutive shots, the entire section is exempt from the test. If the student misses, the next student plays the next corresponding scale in the circle of fifths.

Balance and Blend
Heath and Christine agree that balance is the ability to hear all of the instruments in the ensemble clearly. Blend, however, is the ability of an entire section to sound like one instrument. In rehearsal, Heath will first balance each of the section leaders and once there is clarity, ask the other players to match the volume, tone, and intonation of the section leader. "We have the section leaders play the chorale, listening to the tuba and lowest voices. I then ask the students a series of questions to guide their ears and adjust their playing towards the balance I want," Heath said.

To teach students about ensemble blend, Heath and Christine use an exercise they learned from Steve Tyndall, a band director in Georgia, in which two students play half-notes back and forth on one pitch and continue adjusting until the two timbres sound alike. "Students quickly pick up on the differences, and I think the process of experimentation and using their ears to adjust is essential when playing in the ensemble," Heath said.

Both Heath and Christine also use a "passing fours" exercise to teach ensemble blend. This exercise begins with the tubas and continues in reverse score order. Each section sustains one pitch for four counts and passes it to the next section. The purpose is to match intonation, tone, dynamics, attacks, and releases to create a unified section sound. Heath and Christine will use this exercise on any fundamental technique, rhythm sheet, or excerpt of music.

Musicianship
"Musicianship must be the director's priority if it is going to happen," Christine said. "If you think it is important for students to play with a mature style and range of dynamics, then they will," Heath added. Heath and Christine use chorales to teach concepts related to musicianship, such as dynamics and phrase direction. Heath explained:

> We will play a chorale, adding various dynamics and phrase direction, and play it again with no dynamics, or what I call "mezzo-boring." I ask the students what they preferred, and they, of course, say the first one. They see, hear, and enjoy it more when they play with contrast and phrasing. I encourage them to play like that all the time, even if it is not exactly what I want.

"We have to put the impetus on the students," Christine said. "This makes them more aware of the musical possibilities that exist and encourages them to make decisions for themselves."

Words of Wisdom
Heath and Christine encourage directors to assess the current ability level of their students and ensembles, teach fundamental concepts to develop those skills, and program music the students can perform successfully. Christine said:

Teach the students where they are at and build motivation through excellent performances. If you do not know the answer, use the internet or ask veteran teachers for help. Be willing to listen to what they say and make the necessary changes.

Heath added:

If we are not happy with what is happening in our band, we start with ourselves. It is our fault, and we do not make excuses. These students are amazing, and the pressure put on them is far more than what we dealt with as teenagers. We want to give our students the best possible musical experience and grow as musicians to their fullest ability, but at the end of the day, we also want them to have fun, enjoy the experience, and love making music.

Recommended Literature

Band directors contributing to this publication recommended their favorite compositions, grades 1–4. Their responses within each category are listed alphabetically by composer. The most popular titles and composers are listed at the end of this section.

KIM BAIN

Grade 1

Spirit of the Stallion	Brian Balmages
Colliding Visions	Brian Balmages
Incantation and Ritual	Brian Balmages
Character	Larry Clark
Suncatcher	James Curnow
Chant and Fire Ritual	Tyler Grant
Defeating the Giant	Rob Grice
Chariot Race	William Owens
Construction Zone	Robert Sheldon
Across the Serengeti	Jack Wilds
Bravado Tango	Jack Wilds
Knightly Procession	Jack Wilds

Grade 2

Escape from the Deep	Brian Balmages
Miles in the Sky	Tyler Grant
Japanese Pictures	Kevin Mixon
Shipwrecked	Ryan Nowlin
Terminal Velocity	Michael Oare
To Dream in Brushstrokes	Michael Oare
Spit-Fire	William Owens
Ash Lawn Echoes	Robert W. Smith
Knights of Destiny	Michael Sweeney
Selkie	Johnnie Vinson

Grade 3

For the New Day Arisen	Steven Barton
Parade of the Wooden Warriors	Adam Gorb
Celtic Ritual	John Higgins
Songs of Old Kentucky	Brant Karrick
Song of the Plains	Pierre La Plante
Lauda	Timothy Miles
Into the Clouds	Richard Saucedo
West Highlands Sojourn	Robert Sheldon
Clouds that Sail in Heaven	Todd Stalter
In tantum lux	Todd Stalter
Joy	Frank Ticheli
Jubilant Flourishes	Travis J. Weller

ERIN COLE

Grade 1

Incantation and Ritual	Brian Balmages
Whirlwind	Jodie Blackshaw
A Quiet Rain	Walter Cummings
Largo from Symphony No. 9	Antonin Dvořák/Vinson
Rising Star	Samuel Hazo
Chasing Clouds of Glory	Andrew Poor
Safari	Michael Vertoske

Grade 2

Haunted Clocks	Brian Balmages
The Royal Regiment	Joseph Compello
A Song for Friends	Larry Daehn
Dancing Snakes	Neil Simon
The Rowan Tree	Randall Standridge
Distant Thunder of the Sacred Forest	Michael Sweeney
Down by the Salley Gardens	Michael Sweeney

Grade 3

Grace Before Sleep	Susan Barr/Wilson
Marche Diabolique	Brian Balmages
Nimrod from Enigma Variations	Edward Elgar/Bocook
Horkstow Grange	Percy Grainger/Sweeney
The Lost Lady Found	Percy Grainger/Sweeney
Rhythm Stand	Jennifer Higdon
Earth Song	Frank Ticheli

Grade 4

Melodious Thunk	David Biedenbender
Children's March	Percy Grainger/Wagner
Perthshire Majesty	Samuel Hazo
Undertow	John Mackey
The Cave You Fear	Michael Markowski
Simple Gifts: Four Shaker Songs	Frank Ticheli
The Seal Lullaby	Eric Whitacre

CHIP DE STEFANO

Grade 1

Majestica	Brian Balmages
Midnight Mission	Brian Balmages
Midnight Sky	Brian Balmages
Nottingham Castle	Larry Daehn
Passacaglia Collins	Michael Dowden
Shepherd's Hey	Percy Grainger/De Stefano
Chorale and Mystic Chant	Timothy Loest
The King's Feast	Kenneth Singleton
Baywood Overture	James Swearingen
Ye Banks and Braes O'Bonnie Doon	Michael Sweeney

Grade 2

Korean Folk Rhapsody	James Curnow
Kentucky 1800	Clare Grundman
Psalm 42	Samuel Hazo
Prospect	Pierre La Plante
The Cave You Fear	Michael Markowski
The Battle Pavane	Tielman Susato/Sweeney
A Renaissance Revel	Tielman Susato/Singleton
Ancient Voices	Michael Sweeney
Celtic Air and Dance	Michael Sweeney
Fa Una Canzona	Orazio Vecchi/Daehn

Grade 3

Prelude and Fugue in B-flat Major	J.S. Bach/Moehlmann
Melodious Thunk	David Biedenbender
Symphony No. 4	Andrew Boysen
Cafe 512	Ryan George
A Renaissance Festival	Claude Gervaise/Singleton
Parade of the Wooden Warriors	Adam Gorb
An Irish Rhapsody	Clare Grundman
On a Hymnsong of Philip Bliss	David Holsinger
American Riversongs	Pierre La Plante
Cajun Folk Songs	Frank Ticheli

Grade 4	
Canarios Fantasia	Douglas Akey
Prelude, Siciliano and Rondo	Malcolm Arnold/Paynter
Summer Dances	Brian Balmages
Chorale and Capriccio	Caesar Giovannini/Robinson
Mass from La Fiesta Mexicana	H. Owen Reed
Pageant	Vincent Persichetti
Fortress	Frank Ticheli
English Folk Song Suite	Ralph Vaughan Williams
Symphonic Dance No. 3, "Fiesta"	Clifton Williams
Chorale and Shaker Dance	John Zdechlik

EILEEN FRAEDRICH

Year 1

Starsplitter Fanfare	Brian Balmages
Slip and Slide	Ralph Ford
Bugler's Dream ·	Paul Lavender
Trumpet Hero	Paul Lavender
Rock-A-Saurus Rex!	Tom Molter
Samba la Bamba	William Owens
Warp Speed	Michael Story
Heroes and Glory	James Swearingen
Power Rock	Michael Sweeney
Cardiff Castle	Mark Williams
Attack of the Cyclops	Mark Williams

Year 2

Over the Rainbow	Harold Arlen/Story
Winter Wonderland	Felix Bernard/Story
Rock to the Max, Mr. Sax	Joseph Compello
25 or 6 to 4	Robert Lamm/Story
Tuba in Cuba	Victor Lopez
Supercalifragilisticexpialidocious	Richard Sherman/Sweeney
The Tempest	Robert W. Smith
Raiders March	John Williams/Bullock
Star Wars	John Williams/Strommen
Happy	Pharrell Williams/Sweeney

CHERYL FLOYD

Grade 1

Chant for Percussion	Andrew Balent
Song for Friends	Larry Daehn
Mystery of the Maya	John Edmondson
Two-Minute Symphony	Bob Margolis
Atlantis	Anne McGinty
Sea Song Trilogy	Anne McGinty
Ironclad	Sean O'Loughlin
Crown Point March	Bruce Pearson
Furioso	Robert W. Smith
Serengeti Dreams	Robert W. Smith

Grade 2

Hypnotic Fireflies	Brian Balmages
Rhythm Machine	Timothy Broege
Korean Folk Rhapsody	James Curnow
Caprice	William Himes
Soldiers' Procession and Sword Dance	Bob Margolis
All the Pretty Little Horses	Anne McGinty
The Red Balloon	Anne McGinty
Three Russian Cameos	William Rhoads
Cumberland Cross	Carl Strommen
Variations on a Sailing Song	Carl Strommen
The Battle Pavane	Tielman Susato/Margolis
Celtic Air and Dance	Michael Sweeney
Joy	Frank Ticheli
Portrait of a Clown	Frank Ticheli

Grade 3

Cradlesong	Steven Barton
For the New Day Arisen	Steven Barton
Hill Country Flourishes	Steven Barton
Liadov Fanfare	Brian Beck
Sinfonia VI	Timothy Broege
Old Churches	Michael Colgrass

Down a Country Lane	Aaron Copland/Patterson
Diamond Tide	Viet Cuong
Variations on Scarborough Fair	Calvin Custer
Snakes!	Thomas Duffy
Tonadillas Suite	Enrique Granados/Ford
American Riversongs	Pierre La Plante
Lightning Field	John Mackey
Renaissance Fair	Bob Margolis
Anitschka	Johan Nijs
Tudor Sketches	William Owens
Charm	Kevin Puts
El Camino Real	Alfred Reed/Longfield
Dancing at Stonehenge	Anthony Suter
Cajun Folk Songs	Frank Ticheli
Shenandoah	Frank Ticheli
Twilight in the Wilderness	Christopher Tucker
Sang!	Dana Wilson
Grade 4	
Variations on a Korean Folk Song	John Barnes Chance
Crystals	Thomas Duffy
Undertow	John Mackey
Courtly Airs and Dances	Ron Nelson
A Longford Legend	Robert Sheldon
Cajun Folk Songs, Set II	Frank Ticheli
Fortress	Frank Ticheli
Simple Gifts	Frank Ticheli
Puszta!	Jan Van der Roost
Rikudim	Jan Van der Roost
Suite Provençal	Jan Van der Roost
Chorale and Shaker Dance	John Zdechlik

CHRIS GLEASON

Grade 0.5

Whirlwind	Jodie Blackshaw

Grade 1

Theme and Variations	Timothy Broege
Declaration and Dance	Larry Clark
As Winds Dance	Samuel Hazo
Psalm 42	Samuel Hazo
A Prehistoric Suite	Paul Jennings
Clouds	Anne McGinty
Ayre and Dance	Bruce Pearson
Castles and Dragons	Todd Stalter
Fires of Mazama	Michael Sweeney

Grade 2

Salvation Is Created	Pavel Chesnokov/Brown
Korean Folk Rhapsody	James Curnow
Song for Friends	Larry Daehn
The Bonsai Tree	Julie Giroux
Pinnacle	Rob Grice
A Childhood Hymn	David Holsinger
Soldiers' Procession & Sword Dance	Bob Margolis
The Red Balloon	Anne McGinty
A Shaker Gift Song	Frank Ticheli

Grade 2.5

Apparitions	Brian Balmages
Moscow 1941	Brian Balmages
Rippling Watercolors	Brian Balmages
The Twittering Machine	Brian Balmages
Shackelford Banks	Jay Bocook
Balladair	Frank Erickson
The Cave You Fear	Michael Markowski
The Road Unknown	Richard Meyer
Joy	Frank Ticheli
Portrait of a Clown	Frank Ticheli

Grade 3	
Rhythm Machine	Timothy Broege
Air for Band	Frank Erickson
Blue and Green Music	Samuel Hazo
On a Hymnsong of Philip Bliss	David Holsinger
American Riversongs	Pierre La Plante
Lightning Field	John Mackey
Abracadabra	Frank Ticheli
Earth Song	Frank Ticheli
Simple Gifts: Four Shaker Songs	Frank Ticheli
Flourish for Wind Band	Ralph Vaughan Williams
Grade 4	
Prelude, Siciliano, and Rondo	Malcolm Arnold/Paynter
Alligator Alley	Michael Daugherty
Overture in B-flat	Caesar Giovaninni
Courtly Airs and Dances	Ron Nelson
The Thunderer	John Philip Sousa
Amazing Grace	Frank Ticheli
I'm Seventeen Come Sunday	Ralph Vaughan Williams
Chorale and Shaker Dance	John Zdechlik

COREY GRAVES

Grade 1

Little Brazil Suite	Andrew Balent
Korean Folk Rhapsody	James Curnow
Phantom Ship	Elliot Del Borgo
Wildwind Overture	John Kinyon
Soldiers' Procession and Sword Dance	Bob Margolis
Atlantis	Anne McGinty
Courtlandt County Festival	William Owens
A Joyful Journey	Robert Sheldon
Sakura	Michael Story
Capriol Suite	Peter Warlock/Longfield

Grade 2

Mosswood Lullaby	Brian Beck
Dolce and Dance	Gary Fagan
A Childhood Hymn	David Holsinger
Japanese Pictures	Kevin Mixon
Highland Legend	John Moss
Crest of Nobility	Robert Sheldon
Irish Air and Dance	Michael Story
Cumberland Cross	Carl Strommen
Blue Ridge Saga	James Swearingen
Greenwillow Portrait	Mark Williams

Grade 3

Deir In De	Warren Barker
Be Thou My Vision	Larry Clark
Variations on Scarborough Fair	Calvin Custer
Australian Up-Country Tune	Percy Grainger/Bainum
Country Gardens	Percy Grainger/Sousa/Brion/ Schissel
On a Hymnsong of Philip Bliss	David Holsinger
J. S. Jig	Brant Karrick
Chanteys	Robert Sheldon
West Highlands Sojourn	Robert Sheldon
Old Scottish Melody	Charles Wiley

Grade 4

Prelude, Siciliano, and Rondo	Malcolm Arnold/Paynter
Incantation and Dance	John Barnes Chance
Variations on a Korean Folk Song	John Barnes Chance
Shepherd's Hey	Percy Grainger/Rogers
Themes from Green Bushes	Percy Grainger/Daehn
Colonial Airs and Dances	Robert Jager
A Longford Legend	Robert Sheldon
Suite Provençal	Jan Van der Roost
Symphonic Dance No. 3, "Fiesta"	Clifton Williams
Chorale and Shaker Dance	John Zdechlik

ROBERT HERRINGS

Grade 1

Little Brazil Suite	Andrew Balent
Dancing Kites	Chris Bernotas
Summit Fanfare	William Owens
Corps of Discovery	William Owens
Egyptique	William Owens
Big Sky Discovery	Robert Sheldon
Plaza de Toros	Michael Story
Sakura	Michael Story
Serengeti Dreams	Robert W. Smith
Capriol Suite	Peter Warlock/Longfield

Grade 2

Blue Ridge Reel	Brian Balmages
Colliding Visions	Brian Balmages
Hypnotic Fireflies	Brian Balmages
Moscow 1941	Brian Balmages
Fireball!	Brian Beck
Our Kingsland Spring	Samuel Hazo
Kenya Contrasts	William Himes
Japanese Pictures	Kevin Mixon
Portsmouth Reflections	Michael Oare
The Rowan Tree	Randall Standridge

Grade 3

Arabian Dances	Brian Balmages
Rippling Watercolors	Brian Balmages
Brookshire Suite	James Barnes
La Madre de Los Gatos	Brian Beck
Variations on Scarborough Fair	Calvin Custer
I'm Seventeen Come Sunday	Percy Grainger
Tonadillas Suite	Enrique Granados/Ford
J. S. Jig	Brant Karrick
A Walk in the Morning Sun	Pierre La Plante
West Highlands Sojourn	Robert Sheldon
Three Ayres from Gloucester	Hugh Stuart

Grade 4	
Ave Maria	Franz Biebl/Cameron
Incantation and Dance	John Barnes Chance
Variations on a Korean Folk Song	John Barnes Chance
Mock Morris	Percy Grainger/Kreines
Shepherd's Hey	Percy Grainger/Rogers
Themes from Green Bushes	Percy Grainger/Daehn
Concord	Clare Grundman
Sheltering Sky	John Mackey
A Jubliant Overture	Alfred Reed
A Longford Legend	Robert Sheldon
Dublin Dances	Jan Van der Roost
Suite Provençal	Jan Van der Roost
Symphonic Dance No. 3, "Fiesta"	Clifton Williams
Arirang and Akatonbo	Kosaku Yamada/Chang Su-Koh
Chorale and Shaker Dance	John Zdechlik

152

CINDY LANSFORD

Grade 1

Bartók Folk Trilogy	Béla Bartók/McGinty
Dancing Kites	Chris Bernotas
Phantom Ship	Elliot del Borgo
Cascadia Celebration	Steve Hodges
The Band in the Square on the 4th of July	Pierre La Plante
Corps of Discovery	William Owens
Pevensey Castle	Robert Sheldon
Medieval Legend	Michael Story
Fanfare for a New Age	Michael Story
Mystery Ride	Terry White

Grade 2

Blue Ridge Reel	Brian Balmages
Colliding Visions	Brian Balmages
Sparks	Brian Balmages
New Horizons	Bruce Corrigan
Our Kingsland Spring	Samuel Hazo
Marching Song	Gustav Holst/Moss
Highland Legend	John Moss
Heaven's Light	Steve Reineke
Joy	Frank Ticheli
Capriol Suite	Peter Warlock/Longfield

Grade 3

Variations on Scarborough Fair	Calvin Custer
Butterfly's Ball	Ryan Fraley
Spiritual from Symphony No 5 1/2	Don Gillis/Bainum
Tonadillas Suite	Enrique Granados/Ford
Voices of the Sky	Samuel Hazo
J. S. Jig	Brant Karrick
A Walk in the Morning Sun	Pierre La Plante
Winter on Emerald Bay	Alan Lee Silva
West Highlands Sojourn	Robert Sheldon
Fortress	Frank Ticheli

Grade 4	
Con Sabor Español	Robert Buckley
Incantation and Dance	John Barnes Chance
Satiric Dances	Norman Dello Joio
Shepherd's Hey	Percy Grainger/Rogers
Concord	Clare Grundman
Colonial Airs and Dances	Robert Jager
Sheltering Sky	John Mackey
Courtly Airs and Dances	Ron Nelson
A Longford Legend	Robert Sheldon
Suite Provençal	Jan Van der Roost

EVERETT McCONN

Grade 1

A Song for Friends	Larry Daehn
Anthem	John Edmonson
Flourish	Sandy Feldstein and Larry Clark
Russian Sailor's Dance	Reinhold Glière/Balent
Jupiter from The Planets	Gustav Holst/Williams
Azure Hills	Steve Hodges
Morning Mist	Robert Sheldon
Imperium	Michael Sweeney
First Light	First Ticheli
Linden Lea	Ralph Vaughan Williams/ Wagner

Grade 2

All Trails Lead West	David Bobrowitz
Sleep Gently, My Child	Johannes Brahms/Mahaffey
Shaker Variants	Elliot Del Borgo
A Childhood Hymn	David Holsinger
Mars	Gustav Holst/Vinson
Appalachian Morning	Robert Sheldon
Black Is the Color	Robert Sheldon
Then I Saw the Lucent Sky	Todd Stalter
Argentum	Randall Standridge

Grade 3

Yorkshire Ballad	James Barnes
Be Thou My Vision	Larry Clark
Down a Country Lane	Aaron Copland/Patterson
Kentucky 1800	Clare Grundman
Novo Lenio	Samuel Hazo
On a Hymnsong of Philip Bliss	David Holsinger
Ritual	Vaclav Nelhybel
Polly Oliver	Thomas Root
La Boutique Fantasque	Gioachino Rossini/Respighi/ Mahaffey

Fall River Overture	Robert Sheldon
Julia Delaney's Reel	Carl Strommen
Simple Gifts: Four Shaker Songs	Frank Ticheli
Grade 4	
Dusk	Steven Bryant
Armida Overture	Franz Joseph Haydn/Bowles
American Riversongs	Pierre La Plante
A Longford Legend	Robert Sheldon
Cajun Folk Songs	Frank Ticheli
Fortress	Frank Ticheli

HEATH AND CHRISTINE WOLF

Grade 1

Dragon Slayer	Rob Grice
A Prehistoric Suite	Paul Jennings
Gateway March	Eric Osterling
Full Circle	Mekel Rogers
Starburst Fanfare	David Shaffer
The Invincible Warrior	David Shaffer
Ceremonium	Robert W. Smith
Celtic Air and Dance	Michael Sweeney

Grade 2

Rain	Brian Balmages
Rippling Watercolors	Brian Balmages
Advance	Larry Clark
The Screaming Eagles	John Edmondson
Devil Dance	John Kinyon
Flight of the Thunderbird	Richard Saucedo
Appalachian Morning	Robert Sheldon
Stargazer	David Shaffer
Yellow	Robert W. Smith
Joy	Frank Ticheli

Grade 3

The Orange Bowl	Henry Fillmore
An Irish Rhapsody	Clare Grundman
Blue and Green Music	Samuel Hazo
First Suite in E-flat	Gustav Holst/Longfield
Brighton Beach	William Latham
Lullaby from a Distant Star	Richard Saucedo
Triumphant Fanfare	Richard Saucedo
Choreography	Robert Sheldon
Klezmer Karnival	Phillip Sparke
Imaginarium	Randall Standridge
Fortress	Frank Ticheli

Grade 4	
Prelude, Siciliano, and Rondo	Malcolm Arnold/Paynter
Americans We	Henry Fillmore
Men of Ohio	Henry Fillmore
The Echo Never Fades	David Gillingham
Sheltering Sky	John Mackey
Galop	Amilcare Ponchielli/Daehn
A Longford Legend	Robert Sheldon

POPULARITY BY TITLE

Listed below, in priority order, are the most popular titles in each category.

Grade 1

Colliding Visions	Brian Balmages
Serengeti Dreams	Robert W. Smith
Corps of Discovery	William Owens
Atlantis	Anne McGinty
Sakura	Michael Story

Grade 2

Korean Folk Rhapsody	James Curnow
Joy	Frank Ticheli
Rippling Watercolors	Brian Balmages
A Childhood Hymn	David Holsinger
Japanese Pictures	Kevin Mixon

Grade 3

American Riversongs	Pierre La Plante
On a Hymnsong of Philip Bliss	David Holsinger
West Highlands Sojourn	Robert Sheldon
Variations on Scarborough Fair	Calvin Custer
J.S. Jig	Brant Karrick

Grade 4

Chorale and Shaker Dance	John Zdechlik
Prelude, Siciliano, and Rondo	Malcolm Arnold/Paynter
Suite Provençal	Jan Van der Roost
Variations on a Korean Folk Song	John Barnes Chance
A Longford Legend	Robert Sheldon

POPULARITY BY COMPOSER

Listed below, in priority order, are the most popular composers in each category.

Grade 1

Michael Story
Michael Sweeney
Brian Balmages
Robert Sheldon
William Owens

Grade 2

Brian Balmages
Frank Ticheli
Anne McGinty
Michael Sweeney
Randall Standridge

Grade 3

Frank Ticheli
Robert Sheldon
Pierre La Plante
Calvin Custer
Brant Karrick

Grade 4

Frank Ticheli
Percy Grainger
Jan Van der Roost
John Barnes Chance
John Mackey

About the Author

Stephen Meyer is the director of bands and assistant professor of music at Northern Arizona University. He previously served on the faculties of the Crane School of Music at SUNY Potsdam and the University of South Carolina. As director of bands at Clear Creek High School in League City, Texas, the Clear Creek Wind Ensemble was a featured ensemble at the 2013 Midwest Clinic and a three-time National Winner in the National Wind Band Honors project.

Prior to Clear Creek, Meyer taught at Harrison High School in Cobb County, Georgia, where he assisted with performances at the Midwest Clinic and the Georgia Music Educators Association. As co-director of the marching band, the ensemble was a Bands of America Regional Champion and Super-Regional Finalist, a Bands of America Grand National Finalist, and a featured ensemble in the Macy's Thanksgiving Day Parade.

Dr. Meyer graduated *magna cum laude* from the Indiana University Jacobs School of Music with a bachelor of music education degree and earned both a master's and doctorate from the University of Michigan. He is also the author of *Rehearsing the High School Band*, published by Meredith Music Publications.